RAMBAN
AS
A GUIDE
TO
TODAY'S PERPLEXED

RAMBAN

AS
A GUIDE
TO
TODAY'S PERPLEXED

MINING
THE
CHUMASH COMMENTARY
FOR HELP
IN
COPING WITH
OUR
TOPSY-TURVY WORLD

MOSHE M. EISEMANN

Rabbi Moshe M. Eisemann
403 Yeshiva Lane, Apt. 1B
Baltimore, MD 21208
(410) 484-7396
www.kishinievyeshiva.org

Design: Misha Beletsky
Typesetting: Jerusalem Typesetting, www.jerusalemtype.com
Editing: Reuven Abedon

This book was set in Adobe Garamond Pro
and NarkisClassicMFO

ISBN: 0-9769161-8-5

10 9 8 7 6 5 4 3 2 1

Distributed by:
Feldheim Publishers
POB 35002, Jerusalem, Israel 91350
200 Airport Executive Park, Nanuet, N.Y. 10954
www.feldheim.com

Printed in the USA

CONTENTS

RABBI AHARON FELDMAN

ROSH HAYESHIVA
NER ISRAEL RABBINICAL COLLEGE
STUDY: 400 MT. WILSON LANE (410) 484-7200
RESIDENCE: 409 YESHIVA LANE (410) 653-9433
FAX (410) 484-3060
BALTIMORE, MARYLAND 21208

פורים דמוקפין תשס"ו

Rabbi Eisemann has deeply influenced the students at Ner Yisroel with his classes for over thirty years. It is therefore a matter of great joy for me to learn that he is now disseminating his teachings in book form where they will be available to the general public.

From the essays I have seen it is clear that they are inspiring and incisive in their analysis of their respective topics, as well as beautifully presented through elegant and masterful writing.

It is my hope that this book will be well received by all lovers of Torah learning and that it will be given all the recognition which it truly deserves.

With respects,

Aharon Feldman

Aharon Feldman
Rosh Yeshivas Ner Yisroel
Baltimore, MD

AN INVITATION

*G*ood answers need good questions if they are going to engage our interest. There is so much stimulation out there that it takes something unusually piquant to bring our intellectual taste buds to life. The ordinary will simply not do. The extraordinary has a chance.

This given, dear Reader, I am truly grateful to you for electing to join me for the journey which we are about to undertake. The fact that you are reading this marks you as an optimist and makes for a promising beginning. However, you are at a disadvantage. You are intrigued and would like to find out where all this will lead. That makes you, within limits, a captive audience. I hope that you will not be disappointed. Let us ask some good questions, some which really rattle our certainties, so that the possibility of finding an answer—perhaps of finding *the* answer—will drive us to interest and from there to involvement and from there to passion.

Passion! Isn't that a beautiful word? In a world in which "cool" is king,
it is not a very popular commodity.
Let us learn to care. Let us learn to live. Let us learn to fly.
Let us learn to love God's Torah,
to love it passionately.
Let us make its pursuit the content of our day,
the goal of our life,
the crown of our accomplishments.
Come! Let us ask good questions and stalk good answers.
Let us learn.
We have far to go.

PREFACE

or as long as I can remember, I have looked to Ramban to guide me through Chumash. I am not foolish enough to suppose that this personal predilection tells any objective truth. I cannot believe that anyone in our generation would arrogate to himself the right to judge among the classical commentators. Still, so it seems to me, most of us feel more attracted to one commentator than to others, and for me the lodestar has always been Ramban.

Perhaps, although when I began learning Ramban seriously I was not yet aware of it, I intuited something of what the great Chasam Sofer had in mind when he wrote (Responsa 6:61), *While the Ramban commentary to Chumash is readily available, there are few who actually study it. This, in spite of the fact that it is one of the most basic Jewish texts. It offers foundations for* EMUNAH *in its fullest sense, it provides the roots for the flowering of true religious experience.*[1] Moreover, in his ethical will he advised his sons to study Ramban's commentary and to teach it to their children. He felt that the commentary was a repository of those elements which undergird the faith commitments of the Jew.[2]

It seems that the Chasam Sofer saw something in Ramban which he did not see in Rashi. This, in spite of the fact that Ramban, in his introductory remarks to Chumash, asserts unequivocally that to Rashi accrues the *mishpat habechorah*, the "right of the firstborn," implying that his own commentary must take a backseat to Rashi's immortal work.

We will resist the temptation to guess where in the Commentary Chasam Sofer found the fundamental truths of which he spoke. I have some candidates in mind but, without much more probing and analysis, they would have to remain mere guesses. We can employ ourselves more usefully.

Rather, I want to use this Preface to explain what I am trying to do in this book.

I once heard from the late great R. Yaakov Kamenetzky זצ"ל that Ramban used his Commentary to present an entire philosophy of Judaism. He, no less than the Rambam, felt the need to give body to the ideas which animated his relationship to the Ribono shel Olam, to the Torah, to Eretz Yisrael and to Klal Yisrael. He felt himself consumed by a holy fire[3] which demanded to be released. He dreamed of energizing and illuminating the lives of the "young men who are drained and exhausted by exile and sorrows."[4] However, while Rambam chose to present his thoughts in the garb of the philosopher, producing the immortal Guide, Ramban decided to walk in the footsteps of the "lions" who had preceded him.[5] He would "learn" a "*parashah* Chumash" and make the written Torah yield its secrets.

R. Kamenetzky's idea fired my imagination. Was it really true, I wondered, that by studying the Commentary carefully and lovingly, new and deeper understanding of *Yiddishkeit* could and therefore would open up? Were there really worlds waiting to be discovered, heights to be scaled and depths to be plumbed?

I decided to give it a try; to approach the Commentary from a broader perspective. Rather than learn an individual Ramban on an individual *pasuk*, I would, to the extent that it lay within my ability, shoot for the entire *sugia*, range as far as I was able, and, by wedding many different comments into an integrated whole, begin to pin down a *shitah*, a coherent philosophy which would allow me to apprehend a Judaism of which, till now, I had been ignorant.

I chose to explore Ramban's ideas about the nature of man (chapters 1–10) and of *hashgachah*, God's involvement in human affairs (chapters 11–20). I treated each section as a self-contained unit and did not, as I was researching them, spend much time or thought on how the two might eventually mesh and interact.

That I left for chapter 20 and the Epilogue, which, now that I have written them, seems to me to be the most important part of the book. I did indeed find new dimensions in areas of the Torah which I had long known but never understood as profoundly as I do now. Every-day *mitzvos* sprang to life and were revealed as part of a grand system in which life in the Kingdom of the Ribono shel Olam finds expression.

I meant the strange expression "life in the Kingdom of the Ribono shel Olam" quite literally. I am writing this paragraph on Erev Yom Kippur 5766 and look back upon the nine first days of this year's Aseres Yemei Teshuvah. On Rosh HaShanah we are bound to pronounce the Ribono shel Olam as our king (Rosh HaShanah 16a). In the past I had only the haziest idea of what this really meant in practical terms. I truly believe that having studied the ideas of the Ramban with which I deal in this book and having thought the whole thing through as I laid it down in the Epilogue, I have, to some extent, penetrated to the true meaning of this exercise.

It has been a heady experience. Come, join me in the search.

PART I.
RAMBAN
ON
THE NATURE
OF
MAN

*T*he Torah demands that we be good. The Torah demands that we be straight. The Torah demands that we be holy. All in all, the Torah expects a great deal from us. But, needless to say, the Torah does not ask that we perform miracles. There are limits. The impossible, by definition, is not possible.

Simple, isn't it?

Is it? Could it be that these comfortable assumptions miss the mark of Judaism? Could it be that, against all logic and all instinct, the Ribono shel Olam really wants us to be miracle workers?

I will throw a question at you, one which meets the criteria which we set down in the Invitation with which we began this book. Let us take it slowly and carefully. Much depends upon our understanding the question correctly.

We will go to *parashas* Nitzavim (Devarim 30:5–6).

ה. **והביאך יקוק אלהיך אל הארץ אשר ירשו אבתיך** וירשתה והיטבך והרבך מאבתיך:

ו. **ומל יקוק אלהיך את לבבך ואת לבב זרעך** לאהבה את יקוק אלהיך בכל לבבך ובכל נפשך למען חייך.

5. God your Lord will then bring you to the land that your ancestors occupied and you too will occupy it. God will be good to you and make you flourish even more than your ancestors.

6. *God will remove the barriers from your heart and from the hearts of your descendants* so that you will love God your Lord with all your heart and soul. Thus will you be truly alive.

The passage transports us to the heady days of the Messianic future. It promises a time when we will have finally persuaded our hearts of stone to melt a little. We will have become receptive to the whispering voice which will speak to us of a hope which we

3

had long denied ourselves. It will speak to us of the possibility of regeneration which always seemed to us more pipe dream than reality. This will be the moment for which the Ribono shel Olam had always hoped. He will be there to scoop us up in His embrace and to bring us home.

Then what happens? What will make us believe that we are not simply experiencing a small and temporary hiccup, one of the many ups and downs dotting the graph which records our checkered history? Maybe this great moment, like so many others, will soon be followed by a disastrous plunge?

Verse 6 provides the answer, although it loses a great deal in translation. If we are going to stick to conventional English, "remove the barriers from your heart" is probably the best that we can do, because in English the verb *to circumcise* is used only for the physical removal of the foreskin. It does not really carry the metaphorical meaning which we know from the Hebrew.[1]

Still, this rendering certainly attenuates the robust and much more vital *u'mal*. This is not only a matter of style. While removing barriers can be a fairly tame affair, the root word *mul* from which *u'mal* derives carries an unambiguous denotation of a no-holds-barred "cutting off."[2] No benign removal, this. Some very profound change in our very being is implied.

So, if we decide to ignore correct English usage and say what we want to say and how we really want to say it, this is how it will sound. The peak of the Messianic era, the high point which will occur only after the Ribono shel Olam will have brought us back home, will involve a drastic piece of surgery. God will "cut out" something from our hearts, a blockage which until then had never permitted us access to true love of the Ribono shel Olam.

Let us go to the Ramban and find out what this is all about.

ו. **ומל ה' אלהיך את לבבך**–זהו שאמרו (שבת קד א) הבא לטהר מסייעין אותו, מבטיחך שתשוב אליו בכל לבבך והוא יעזור אותך. ונראה מן הכתובים ענין זה שאומר, כי מזמן הבריאה היתה רשות ביד האדם לעשות כרצונו צדיק או רשע, וכל זמן התורה כן, כדי שיהיה להם זכות בבחירתם בטוב ועונש ברצותם ברע. אבל לימות המשיח, תהיה הבחירה בטוב להם טבע, לא יתאוה להם הלב למה שאינו ראוי ולא יחפוץ בו כלל. והיא המילה הנזכרת כאן. כי החמדה

והתאוה ערלה ללב, ומול הלב הוא שלא יחמוד ולא יתאוה. וישוב האדם בזמן
ההוא לאשר היה קודם חטאו של אדם הראשון, שהיה עושה בטבעו מה שראוי
לעשות ולא היה לו ברצונו דבר והפכו...

6. AND HASHEM YOUR GOD WILL CIRCUMCISE YOUR
HEART: This idea accords with the teaching of the Sages that
a helping hand from heaven will be stretched out to anyone
who sincerely wants to improve. Moshe Rabbeinu is promising us that one day we will want to return to God and that
He will help us. . . .

Throughout history, starting from the moment of Creation,
man has had the power to do as he pleased, to be righteous
or wicked. The purpose of this gift of *bechirah*, free choice,
was to allow people to gain merit upon choosing good and
deserve punishment for preferring evil. All this will change
when Moshiach comes. Our very nature will incline us to do
only what is good; there will be no inclination at all towards
anything that is improper.

This is the "circumcision" mentioned here, for lust and desire are the "foreskin" of the heart. "Circumcision of the heart"
means that from now on one's heart will not covet or desire
evil. *Man will return at that time to what he was before the sin
of Adam, when he naturally did what should properly be done,
and he was never conflicted by contradictory urges.* . . .

These are miracles of significant proportions. A return to Eden—
that is no small matter. God, we might almost say, will finally have
it His way. This is how He had wanted man to be. This is how it
would have been had Adam decided not to eat from the forbidden fruit. It will have taken a long time. But, in the end, we will
be what we were always meant to be. It will be as natural for us
to strive for goodness as it is for the lion to roar, the snake to bite,
the wind to blow and the rain to fall. Man will finally stop acting
as the only killjoy in nature, the only one who decides, perversely,
to sing out of tune.

It is a beguiling picture. We can close our eyes and dream about
it. In our mind we file it together with Yeshayahu's vision of sheep
and wolf living peacefully together. There is much beauty, much

peace which the future promises us. But, dreams are for the night. With morning, reality sets in. And the world we know is a cantankerous one. There is biting and tearing, pecking and gouging and blood and tears and death and decay. And most certainly we are not naturally good. What dreadful battles we have to fight! How frequently we lie vanquished, wallowing in the cloying filth of our failures.

So, do not speak to us of the circumcision of the heart in the present tense. People who dream while they are crossing the street are in for a lot of trouble.

So what are we to do with Devarim 10:16? There Moshe Rabbeinu exhorts us in real terms, in the here and now, *Remove the barriers from your hearts.*[3] What can he possibly mean? How are we to go about "circumcising" our hearts? Are we to generate the same miraculous renewal[4] which God promises to bring about in the Messianic age? Are we then to become miracle workers?

This is the question which I promised you, dear Reader. Let us spell it out.

> How are we to understand the charge that we are to "circumcise" our own hearts, when "circumcision" of the heart is so plainly something which requires the Ribono shel Olam's intervention?
>
> How can we, with all our frailties, be expected to bring about a mini Messianic era?[5]

This seems to be a major problem, does it not?

Before we embark upon our journey of discovery, a word is in place concerning the goal which I had in mind when writing this book and concerning the way in which it is organized.

As the title implies, I wanted to learn from the Ramban's Torah Commentary what I was supposed to do with my life. We all know that R. Moshe Chaim Luzzatto taught us that before we can expect any progress,[6] we must know clearly what is expected of us[7] and, having discovered that, we are to internalize this knowledge so that, for ourselves at least, it becomes the beacon of truth[8] which we are to follow (Mesilas Yesharim, chapter 1).[9] I knew then, and know it better now, that this is a tall order. Still, something told me that I should try.

In studying Ramban's commentary to the Chumash, I noticed that, on many fundamental issues, his ideas are spread over a number of different comments. I discovered soon enough that all of these must be considered together if we are to be able to speak with any authority or even clarity.

When I began to write, I had dreams of tackling a number of different subjects. As I went along I stumbled upon so many complexities that in the end I was able to include only two issues, and those, without any sense that I have penetrated beyond the surface. The one concerns the creation of man and what we may conclude concerning his obligations towards the Ribono shel Olam, his duties towards his fellows, and those which he owes himself. The second deals with God's *hashgachah*, the providential care which He bestows upon His creation in general and upon His people, Klal Yisrael, in particular.

The study of these two subjects comprises the first two sections of this book. In the third section I attempt to pull the two together and draw some practical conclusions.

The question which we have raised in this chapter belongs in the first section and will be resolved in chapter 10.

Come, let us set out on our journey of discovery. We have far to go!

e started off the previous chapter by stating a truism which we had supposed should cause us no trouble at all. We said that the impossible is by definition not possible. By the time we reached the end of the chapter, our earlier certainty had lost its conviction.

Somewhere within our drab, pedestrian selves a miracle worker seems to be hidden. If we are to find him we must become better acquainted with man, that strange intruder into God's otherwise predictable world. Man, the only one among God's creatures in whom heaven and earth meet, kiss[1]—and explode into countless unpredictable shapes, some grotesque and terrifying, others of aching beauty. Perhaps the concept of the "impossible" belongs in a more prosaic world.

Dear Reader: at this point I am going to share some secrets with you concerning the writer's craft, at least to the extent that my own experiences have allowed me to draw some conclusions. Sometimes it is plodding and frustrating work. Words keep slipping out of your grasp; sentences are cranky and refuse to fall into shape. If, when this happens, you ignore the trouble signs and keep on writing, you will find yourself, as I have often found myself, doing a lot of erasing.

At other times, though, ideas seem to find their own energy. They cannot wait to grab you by the lapels, to sweep you along by the music of their cadences, the power of their phrasing, the sheer rightness of what they have to communicate.

The formulation which I used in the last paragraph, the picture of man as a complex unit in whom heaven and earth meet and "kiss," belongs to this latter category. It more or less produced itself and, as I wrote it, I felt myself to be more secretary than author. We will be returning to the idea of the kiss, and I plan to examine its ramifications closely. Keep it in mind, dear Reader, it is a strong image and may just remain with you long after much else that you will read in this book will have been forgotten.

So, let us begin at the beginning.

Bereishis 1:26 introduces the creation of man with the words *Let us make man in OUR form and in OUR likeness.*[2] The use of the plural form, *let Us make man,* clearly requires an explanation.[3] Here, together with a paraphrase, is how Ramban deals with the issue.

והפשט הנכון במלת "נעשה" הוא, מפני שכבר הראית לדעת (לעיל פסוק א)
כי האלהים ברא יש מאין ביום הראשון לבדו, ואחר כך מן היסודות ההם
הנבראים יצר ועשה. וכאשר נתן במים כח השרוץ לשרוץ נפש חיה והיה
המאמר בהם "ישרצו המים", והיה המאמר בבהמה "תוצא הארץ", אמר
באדם "נעשה", כלומר אני והארץ הנזכרת נעשה אדם, שתוציא הארץ הגוף
מיסודיה כאשר עשתה בבהמה ובחיה, כדכתיב (להלן ב ז) וייצר ה' אלהים
את האדם עפר מן האדמה, ויתן הוא יתברך הרוח מפי עליון, כדכתיב (שם)
ויפח באפיו נשמת חיים:

The creation of man is to be a partnership between the earth and God. Ramban spells out what each of them will provide. Here is the phrase which should engage our attention. *That the earth, from its elements, should bring forth the* guf *(body) as it did for the animals . . . and that He should provide the* ru'ach *(spirit) with His own breath.*

Here is a chart to help us along.

That THE EARTH from its elements should bring forth,	the GUF as it did for both the domesticated and the undomesticated animals.
HE, BLESSED BE HIS NAME, should give.	the RU'ACH from the mouth of the Most High.

Let us see what we have here.

1. Man has a body; so do the animals.

2. Man is alive (*ru'ach*), that is, he moves, he breathes, he eats, he digests, he procreates; so do the animals.

3. Man has an intellect, he has an emotional life, he has the capacity to appreciate beauty, he can laugh and he can cry, he has an appreciation for the holy; animals have none of these.

For simplicity's sake, let us call the middle level (2) a *life force* and the third one (3) a *soul*.

Here is a question. Who provides the life force? Is it the earth or is it God? Put differently: Can *guf* be expanded to mean not only the *body* but also the *life force*? Or, if that cannot be done, can *ru'ach* be expanded to include not only the *soul* but also the *life force*?

Here is an excerpt from Ramban to Bereishis 1:26:

יצירת האדם ברוחו, הוא **הנפש אשר בדם** נעשה מן הארץ כמאמר החיה
והבהמה, כי כל נפשות התנועה נעשו יחד, ואחר כן ברא להם גופות, עשה
תחילה גופי הבהמה והחיה, ואחר כך גוף האדם, ונתן בו הנפש הזו, ואחר כן
נפח בו נשמה עליונית, כי הנפש הנפרדת אשר בו, היא שנתיחד בה מאמר אחר
אל האלהים אשר נתנה, כדכתיב (להלן ב ז) ויפח באפיו נשמת חיים:

Man, together with the life force which resides in his blood,[4] was made from the earth just as was the case with all the animals. All life forces, those of animals and those of man, were created together. Once these existed God called forth the bodies, those of the animals and that of man, and injected them with the appropriate life force. Only after all this was done did God imbue man with his soul, brought down from the upper spheres.

Very clearly, for both animals and man, the life force emanated from the earth. Before God imbued man with his soul, man was a living, sentient being though not yet in any way human. God took a living brute and turned him into a man.[5]

H ave you ever thought deeply about bread? We take it pretty much for granted; why shouldn't we? And yet, few things are ever quite as simple as they appear to be. A time came in Adam's life when bread mattered more than anything else in the world. He needed it, needed it desperately, to bolster his sagging self-esteem, wipe tears of despair from his eyes and make it possible to face life outside Eden with renewed hope.

Here is what happened, as recounted in Yalkut Shimoni, Bereishis 32.

אמר ריש לקיש, בשעה שא"ל הקב"ל לאדם הראשון, "וקוץ ודרדר תצמיח
לך!" זלגו עיניו דמעות. אמר לפניו "רבש"ע, אני וחמורי נאכל **באבוס אחד**?"
כיון שא"ל, "בזעת אפיך תאכל **לחם**." נתקררה דעתו.

Reish Lakish taught: when God told Adam that [outside Gan Eden] he would have to battle the thorns and thistles and that then he would eat *the grass of the field,* he burst into tears. He said, "Master of the universe, am I and my donkey then to eat out of the same trough?" When God continued, "You shall eat *bread* by the sweat of your brow," he felt relieved.

Adam was horrified at the thought that he was to eat the earth's vegetation "as is." What, then, would differentiate him from his donkey? When God promised that he would be eating not grass but bread, his fears were dispelled. Bread does not grow; it is made. Human initiative is required and human skills are brought into play. That is a different story altogether.

Why?

Obviously, we are after bigger game than simply a loaf of bread. I wonder what Adam felt about the fact that he was created on the sixth day, the very day upon which the animals were created. Does this not imply some measure of congruence?[1] If eating from the same trough as his donkey caused him so much anguish, would not the implications of this apparent blurring of distinctions have concerned him even more?[2]

How are we to understand the dispositions which the Ribono shel Olam made for the fifth and sixth days of Creation? Would we not have supposed that animals have more in common with the fish and the fowl which came into being on the fifth day, than with man, created in the "image"[3] of God on the sixth?

We are going to have to study a little Hebrew. We will use Ramban on Bereishis 1:1 as our guide.

Three verbs recur constantly in the Creation narrative and we need to sort them out. They are *bara*, to create; *yatzar*, to form; and *asah*, to make. In this threesome *bara* stands on its own; the other two belong together. *Bara* is the only word in Hebrew which describes creating something out of nothing. The other two assume the prior existence of a material out of which things can be *formed* or *made*.

Ramban posits that nothing in nature was created *ex nihilo*. Rather, before anything else came into being, God created a *hylic*[4] "something" which had no substance of its own but contained within itself infinite potential. This *hyle* was the raw material from which God *formed* or *made* everything else. When Bereishis 1:1 speaks of *bara*, it has this *hyle* in mind. It alone was actually created by God.

Ramban's definition of *bara* seems to run into trouble in two instances. Bereishis 1:21 reads, *God created* (bara) *the vast sea monsters*, and Bereishis 2:27 reads, *God created* (bara) *the man*. If everything was *formed* or *made* from the already existing primordial *hylic* "something," why use *bara* when talking about the sea monsters and man?

Ramban himself raises the question. Here is a quote together with a paraphrase.

ויברא אלהים את התנינים הגדולים–בעבור גודל הנבראים האלה שיש מהם
אורכם פרסאות רבות, הגידו היונים בספריהם שידעו מהם ארוכים חמש
מאות פרסה, ורבותינו גם כן הפליגו בהם (עיין ב"ב עג ב), בעבור זה ייחס
בהם הבריאה לאלהים, כי הוא שהמציאם מאין מבראשית, כאשר פירשתי

לשון בריאה (לעיל פסוק א). וכן יעשה באדם למעלתו, להודיע כי הוא מוצא מאין עם דעתו ושכלו .

The sea monsters are huge beyond anything that can be imagined. Some of them are many leagues in length. Greek scientists speak of encountering such as measure five hundred leagues. Such mammoths can only have been literally "created" by God. It can only be He who brought them forth out of nothing.

The same is true concerning man. Man is unique not because of his enormous physical size but because of his ascendancy over the rest of nature. The Torah uses *bara* to tell us that the human element in man was brought forth from nothingness. The most versatile *hyle* could never have generated man's mind.

We explained earlier that the *hylic* "something" which God brought forth from nothing had no substance but contained within itself infinite potential. In the light of what Ramban says here, we must modify the term "infinite" just a little. There were indeed no limits for what the *hyle* could produce *within nature*. Now nature certainly contains huge bodies, many times bigger than five hundred leagues. We need only think of the mighty stars and the unimaginable distances between them to realize that nature has nothing to fear from size. However, to qualify as "natural" a certain measured progression is required. The flea and the elephant can companionably occupy the same earth because between the one and the other there are millions of creatures, each only slightly larger than the one before it. There are no unexpected breaks. The same is true for the heavenly bodies. Existence up there, it is true, is measured in light-years, but situated between galaxies closest to Earth and farthest away are those of medium distance, creating an unbroken continuum.

However, for a monster spanning five hundred leagues, there is simply no allowance in the earthly system. Such a creature is totally out of proportion to everything else. It cannot be part of the "nature" which we experience on Earth and because of that it cannot have been part of the *hylic* potential. If they existed at all, it could only have been because God called them forth from the bottomless nothingness which preceded existence.

The same is true for man. There simply is nothing in the universe to which his humanity could be considered even a distant cousin. He is *sui generis*, an intruder into the otherwise interlocking relationships which trace their lineage to the *hylic* potential. He can have come from nowhere but from God's will to grasp into the infinite "nothing" and draw out His most beloved child.

Let us now look at Bereishis 1:27 a little more closely.

ויברא אל־הים את האדם בצלמו, בצלם אל־הים ברא אותו.

Then God created man in His *tzelem*, in the *tzelem of God He created him.*

For the moment, we have left *tzelem* untranslated. We will need to do a little more research if we are to find a really good rendering for this pivotal word.

The focus of our interest will be Bereishis 1:26, a verse which we have already discussed in chapter 2. The verse reads, *Let Us make man in Our* TZELEM *and in Our* DEMUS. In the previous chapter we discussed the plural, *Let Us make.* We noted that Ramban has God addressing the earth. *Let the two of us together make man.* This is as far as we went in chapter 2. We did not make the point, but need to make it now, that from this interpretation of the plural *Let us make*, it follows that the plural, *in* OUR TZELEM and *in* OUR DEMUS, must also refer to both God and the earth. Man is to be created in the *tzelem* and *demus* of both God and the earth.

This point is made by Ramban in his commentary to verse 26. Here is how he puts it:

ואמר בצלמנו כדמותנו–כי ידמה לשניהם, במתכונת גופו לארץ אשר לוקח
ממנה, וידמה ברוח לעליונים, שאינה גוף ולא תמות.

The plural, *in* OUR TZELEM *and in* OUR DEMUS, is used because man is to be similar to both God and the earth. He will be similar to the earth from which he was produced in the way that his body is constructed. His spiritual essence will resemble the upper realms as it is incorporeal and immortal.

At this point Ramban has not yet defined the meaning of *tzelem*.[5]

We will not quote the following Ramban verbatim because most of the piece is taken up with citations which support his definition. We will satisfy ourselves by noting that he equates *tzelem* with *to'ar*. Now, *to'ar* itself is not easy to translate. At the most basic level it seems to describe a quality which draws attention to itself, hence the verbal form *leta'er*, to describe. Beginning in medieval times, the use of "*to'ar*" as an adjective, "to describe" a noun came into use. Thus, we could say that *to'ar* would be any property which in some way defines a given object in the eyes of the beholder.

Here is an excerpt from the Ramban where he describes in what way man is marked by the *tzelem* of God.

הנה האדם דומה . . . לעליונים בתאר ו"הדר" כדכתיב, וכבוד והדר תעטרהו,
והוא מגמת פניו בחכמה ובדעת וכשרון המעשה.

Now man does indeed have the identifying features of the *upper ones*, meaning the nonphysical world, which is expressed in *hadar*, beauty, as it says in Tehilim 8:6, *You have crowned him with glory and with beauty.* This *hadar* is expressed in a face oriented towards its goals with wisdom, good sense and well thought-out actions.

There really is something Godlike in man.

Taking everything which we have learned together, we are now able to have a better grasp of the whole picture. We noted above that the Torah uses *bara* when describing the creation of man (Bereishis 1:27); Ramban felt the need to address this usage since it appeared to contradict his definition of the verb. He reconciled the contradiction by saying that man could not possibly have been produced from the *hylic* "something" because he stands completely outside anything that can be defined as nature.

Now let us take another look at this verse, *God created man in His* TZELEM, *in the* TZELEM *of God did He create him.* We note that the verse speaks only of that aspect of man which is created in God's *tzelem*, not that part of him in which he shares earth's *tzelem*.[6] Clearly the earthly *tzelem* does not require *creatio ex nihilo* but can find its source in the *hylic* "something."

We asked before why the Ribono shel Olam would have wanted to create man on the same day that He created the animals. We wondered why Adam, who had agonized about feeding from the same trough as his donkey, was not hurt that he was created on the same day as the animals.

Man coming into existence on the same day as the animals now becomes logical indeed. The *tzelem* which he shares with the earth is produced from the *hylic* "something" in precisely the same way in which the animals were produced. As far as his earthly *tzelem* is concerned, man is, in fact, very much cousin to the animals. It is the heavenly *tzelem* of man that makes him so special.

Adam found no reason to complain that he was created on Friday. Why, then, was the thought that he would have to share his donkey's trough so painful to him? What comfort did he find in the knowledge that, after all, he would be eating man-made bread?

We have come to the very crux of the human dilemma. The dénouement of the problem deserves a chapter of its own.

Come, let us learn.

4: A KISS THAT CAN CHANGE A LIFE

*I*n chapter 2 we described man as that strange intruder into God's otherwise predictable world, the only one among God's creatures in whom heaven and earth meet and kiss.

Let us think a little about kissing.[1] What exactly are we doing when we kiss somebody?

Mishlei 24:26 may hold the key. Here is a very loose translation: *A cogent argument will cause the lips [of anyone who would have been inclined to disagree] to kiss.*[2] Lips kissing is used as a metaphor for remaining silent, that is, for closing one's mouth. The act of kissing is viewed as a coming together.[3]

Now Yechezkel 37:17 can teach us that when things are brought close enough to each other, a melding can take place which results in the two objects merging into one. The prophet was bidden to take two pieces of wood and to inscribe one with the name Yehudah and the other with the name Yosef. He was to bring the two pieces together to symbolize the ultimate reconciliation between the Northern and Southern kingdoms. The verse reads: *Now bring them close to each other so that they become as one to you, and they will become one entity in your hands.*[4]

We are now ready to examine *hashakah*,[5] the act of joining two bodies of water to each other so that they "kiss." This act has specific halachic ramifications.

For example, we find an application in the law that addresses the making of a *mikveh*. Specific laws govern how the water of a *mikveh* is to be gathered. The details are not important for our present discussion. Suffice it to say that, once a kosher *mikveh* exists, water which would otherwise have been disqualified can be remedied by having it "kiss" the existing *mikveh*. Once the two waters have touched each other, the deficiency is rectified because we view the deficient water as having been blended into the kosher *mikveh*.

The same is true of water which in one way or another has

become *tameh*, ritually defiled. Just as a person or object can be purified through submersion in a *mikveh*, so too *tameh* water can be cleansed through "kissing" the waters of the *mikveh*. Once the waters have touched, purity has been achieved because the *tameh* waters have become part of the *mikveh*. One of the salient features of a *mikveh* is that it cannot be defiled.

In both these cases the *mikveh* water trumps. The impure water does not undermine the efficacy of the already kosher *mikveh*, nor does it impart its impurity. As a result of the "kiss," for reasons that need not detain us here, the *mikveh* draws the less well endowed water into the ambit of its *kashruth* or purity.

What if the two entities which "kiss" each other are equally powerful? Can a melding take place under such circumstances?

That, precisely, is the situation when the earthly and heavenly components present in man meet. In chapter 2 we wrote that when that happens they can explode into countless unpredictable shapes—some grotesque and terrifying, others of aching beauty. Man's capacity for free choice becomes the great arbiter. He decides who or what he is going to be.

Both extremes are possible. The body can be freed of its churlish physicality and blend utterly into the gossamer world in which the soul ranges free. However, things can also work the other way. The soul can be brutalized and become a denizen of the farmyard.

Ramban introduces us to both possibilities.

Let us begin with the second one and work ourselves upwards from there.

Bereishis 6:3 tells how God decided that after an initial grace period of one hundred and twenty years, He would wipe out mankind with the flood. *In as much as man, too, is flesh, My patience with him will not be without limits. He has only another one hundred and twenty years.*

What exactly does *in as much as he too is flesh* mean? Ramban writes as follows:

והנכון בעיני, כי יאמר לא יעמוד רוחי באדם לעולם, בעבור שגם האדם הוא בשר ככל בשר הרומש על הארץ בעוף ובבהמה ובחיה, ואיננו ראוי להיות רוח אלהים בקרבו. והענין לומר, כי האלהים עשה את האדם ישר להיותו כמלאכי

השרת בנפש שנתן בו, והנה נמשך אחרי הבשר ובתאוות הגופניות נמשל
כבהמות נדמו, ולכן לא **ידון** עוד רוח אלהים בקרבו, כי הוא גופני לא אלהי.
It seems to me that the meaning is as follows. My spirit will
not remain in man forever because man also is flesh . . . and
does not deserve to have God's spirit within him. The explanation is as follows: God, by investing man with a soul, had
raised him to a level that was like that of the *mal'achim*, the
spiritual denizens of a spiritual world. But, he was drawn after
the flesh and has become just like any other animal. Having
become corporeal rather than Godly, he cannot expect My
patience to be without limits.

The soul as an outpost from heaven had disappeared. It had been
totally absorbed into the body. Man had become a member in good
standing of the animal world.

Ramban to VaYikra 18:4 provides an example of what can happen at the other end of the spectrum. VaYikra 18:5 promises life[6] in
return for conscientious fulfillment of God's commands. Ramban
believes that the quality of life earned will be determined by the
motivation behind the effort. For example, if someone was metic-
ulous in the fulfillment of *mitzvos* because he was attracted by the
Torah's promise of wealth, health and success in this world, it will
be in that currency that his reward will be paid out. More worthy
considerations will elicit a commensurate reward.

Ramban's description of the fourth and highest level of motivation together with its paraphrasing reads as follows:

והעוזבים כל עניני העולם הזה ואינם משגיחים עליו כאילו אינם בעלי גוף, וכל
מחשבתם וכוונתם בבוראם בלבד כענין באליהו, בהדבק נפשם בשם הנכבד,
יחיו לעד בגופם ובנפשם . . .
Those who care nothing for the physical world, cleaving to
God and acting as though they were not at all corporeal . . .
will live forever, their bodies together with their souls . . .

Ramban could not have been more explicit. Even the body is ame-
nable to sublimation. Drain it of its dross and it will feel at home
in the Olam HaEmes.

Now, clearly, the two examples which we have cited represent two extremes. They are clear and unclouded. Closer to the center, nothing is as unambiguous. There we have constant struggles for supremacy. As in most battles, fortunes will change. Even in the short run, it is hard to know who might be considered a victor and who the vanquished.

Still, all of us yearn for self-knowledge. Who, in the end, are we?

Here, I believe, we have the key to understanding Adam's distress when he thought that he was destined to eat from the same trough as his donkey. He felt condemned to plod through life as simply one more link in the food chain.

His spirits lifted when God told him in the next verse that he would be eating bread. Just as the *hyle* with all the vast potentialities contained in it was helpless when it came to man's soul, so it cannot, in any way at all, produce a loaf of bread. He would be eating man food, not donkey food. There was a good reason for that. It was now clear that, in God's eyes, his soul would preponderate.

*A*re we cousins to the animals or are we not? One way or another we will have to deal with this issue. In chapter 2 we met up with the rather unsettling thought that Adam may have been alive even before God imbued him with the soul which made him human. His vitality at that early stage would have been drawn from the earth together with his body. It would have expressed itself in all the ways in which animals possess faculties which plants do not.

It *is* a strange idea, is it not? It is certainly not what we were taught in Cheder. Still, if we are going to take our Chumash seriously, we must follow the clues wherever they lead. We will learn that Ramban really believes that this is what happened. Let us allow him to guide us on our road to discovery and, if we are fortunate, to self-discovery.

We must first turn to Ramban's thoughts on Bereishis 2:7, the *locus classicus* for this discussion. The verse reads as follows: *HaShem God formed the man [from] earth taken from the ground, and blew a soul which gifted him with life into his nostrils. Thus man became a living being.*[1]

His comments are long and complex. They are just too cumbersome to lend themselves to a word-for-word translation or even to a detailed paraphrase. However, as the title of this chapter makes clear, our real interest is the *"lamed"* of *"l'nefesh chayah."*[2] A short survey of Ramban's analysis addresses this issue.

The *pasuk* tells us that God created man in two stages:

1. He formed him from earth.
2. He imbued him with a soul which gifted him with life.

Ramban wonders what exactly God formed at the first stage. Was it simply a human figure or was it already then, in some way, animated? Ramban argues that it all depends upon the last phrase, *thus man became a living being*.

Here is how.

Taken literally, this phrase seems to favor the "lifeless figure" option. Man was apparently not a "living being" until God had blown the soul into his nostrils.

Nevertheless, Targum seems to disagree. Everywhere else that *nefesh chayah* occurs in Chumash, he translates literally: *a living being*[3]; here he renders, *a form of life which expresses itself in speech*.[4] There can be only one explanation for this deviation from the norm. Man was already a "living being" before God imbued him with the *soul which gifted him with life*. The life force which he shares with the animal world was already in existence. It was only "humanity," expressed in its most exalted form—the ability to speak—which was missing. The second stage did not quicken a lifeless figure. It made a man out of a brute.

It is in the context of these two options, the literal translation and that adopted by Targum, that Ramban examines the meaning of the *"lamed"* of ʟ*'nefesh chayah*.

Now, in general Hebrew usage, the prepositional prefix *"lamed"* is extremely versatile; it appears in many unexpected places. Though we would associate it most naturally with *direction*[5] or *possession*,[6] it also carries many other meanings.[7] For example, it can indicate a change from one thing to another, as in, *The water will change into blood* (ʟ'dam) *on the dry land*. Now, in the lifeless figure option, this would be the natural meaning of the prefix in ʟ'NEFESH *chayah: thus man* (who had previously been a lifeless clod of earth) *changed* INTO *a living being*.

Targum, however, would not have understood the *lamed* in just this way. We recall that, on his reading, man had already been a *living being* before God imbued him with a soul. Ramban considers two possibilities. In the first we are to take the *lamed* as indicating *possession*. The sense is that once man had been imbued with *a soul which gifted him with life*, the earlier life force became subordinate to this soul. In fact, the earlier life force became *possessed* by it. This means that man is not to be made up of two *equal* faculties, the one material, the other from heaven. The soul is always to preponderate. If man were ever to become completely captive to his physical nature as happened before the *mabul* (see chapter 4), it will be a matter of rebellion against its subservience to the soul, not the simple assertion of a natural right. God and the earth, although partners in the act of creation (see chapter 2), would not be equals.

The second approach takes the *lamed* as we did in the "lifeless figure" option. It points to a complete change. We had thought that this usage would not work for Targum. Ramban suggests that it might. The sense would be that once man became imbued with *a soul which gifted him with life* his entire being as it had existed until this time was transformed by his new persona. Only humanity remained—there was no more commonality with the animal world at all.

It would be interesting to discover which of these two alternatives Ramban favors. We ought to be able to do some sleuthing and see if we can find other discussions in his Commentary unrelated to our passage but in which he apparently assumes one or the other of the two options. We will devote the whole of chapter 9 to the discussion of one such passage. Here we will deal with another one. It comes from VaYikra 17:11 and deals with the Torah's prohibition against eating blood.

Before we begin to analyze this source, we will once more present the three available possibilities. We will assign a number to each one. When, at the end of this chapter we summarize our conclusions, we will refer to the various options by the numbers which we are about to assign. This should make an otherwise complicated discussion much easier to follow. Here are the three possibilities.

1. After Adam was formed from the earth he was a lifeless figure. Only after God imbued him with the soul which gifted him with life, did he spring into life. All the faculties of a living human being began to function at the same moment.[8]
2. After Adam was formed from the earth he was already imbued with a brutish life force. He was alive, possessing all those faculties which he shared with the animals, but he was not yet human. When God imbued him with the *soul which*

gifted him with life, he began to speak. He became human. However, all the "animal" faculties which he had possessed before being imbued with humanity remained as they were. They are essentially brutish. God ordained that they were always to be kept subordinate to the soul which God breathed into him.[9]

3. After Adam was formed from the earth he was already imbued with a brutish life force. He was alive, possessing all those faculties which he shared with the animals, but he was not yet human. When God imbued him with the *soul which gifted him with life*, he began to speak. He became human. Up to this point this is identical to the option which we numbered 2. However, now Ramban suggests that after Adam became human the earlier brutish faculties did not maintain their character. Now they blended into the human soul. It was no longer a matter of *subordination* but of *identification*.

It is my contention that the Ramban which we are about to examine will prove that he favors the second of the three options which we have now delineated. The animal life force which preceded the human soul would remain just that. It continued to be a brutish life force even after Adam had been imbued with a human soul. However, it was to be subordinated to the human element within Adam.

Here is the Ramban:

והראוי שנפרש בטעם איסורו, כי השם ברא כל הנבראים התחתונים לצורך האדם כי הוא לבדו בהם מכיר את בוראו, ואף ע"פ כן לא התיר להם באכילה מתחילה רק הצומח לא בעלי הנפש, כאשר בא בפרשת בראשית שנאמר (בראשית א כט) הנה נתתי לכם את כל עשב זורע זרע וגו' . וכאשר היה במבול שנצולו בזכותו של נח והקריב מהם קרבן והיה לרצון לו התיר להם השחיטה, כמו שאמר (שם ט ג) כל רמש אשר הוא חי לכם יהיה לאכלה כירק עשב נתתי לכם את כל, כי חיותם בעבור האדם. והנה התיר גופם אשר הוא חי בעבור האדם, שיהיה להנאתו ולצרכו של אדם, ושתהיה הנפש שבהם לכפרה לאדם, בקרבים לפניו יתברך, לא שיאכלוהו. כי אין לבעל נפש שיאכל נפש, כי הנפשות כולן לאל, הנה כנפש האדם וכנפש הבהמה לו הנה ומקרה אחד להם כמות זה כן מות זה ורוח אחד לכל (קהלת ג יט):

24

Here is a paraphrase:

> We begin with the assumption that all the lower creatures
> were created to serve man's purpose. He stands at the peak of
> creation because only he recognizes his Creator. Nevertheless,
> man was not originally allowed to eat meat. This changed only
> after the Flood when those animals which survived owed their
> lives to Noach. However, even then God allowed him only
> the flesh of these lower creatures, not their blood.
>
> Here is why. Life, all of life including that of the animals,
> belongs to God. Eating meat can be countenanced; eating the
> animal's life force cannot.

This quote is only a small fraction of what the Ramban has to say
about the blood prohibition mentioned in that chapter. To keep
things simple, I will give an accounting of some of the salient
points.

Ramban's point of departure is that the life force of the animal
inheres in the blood.[10] Now there is a significant congruence between the life force of which the animals are possessed and that
which animates man. Take the instinctive loyalty with which dogs
relate to their owners. These characteristics reside in the blood and
are common to both animal and man. If we were allowed to eat the
blood, these faculties which are common to both animal and man
would attach themselves to the human faculties. This would result
in a thickening and coarsening of the human life force closely approaching the nature of the animal.

It seems to me that Ramban's ideas as they are expressed here
can only be understood according to the second of the three options which we have just enumerated. According to the first of these
options there never was an animal-like life force which animated
man. Until God imbued him with the *soul which gifted him with
life*, he was a lifeless figure. After that he was wholly human. According to the third option which we have just enumerated, it is
true that originally he was animated by the animal-like life force
which had been part of the body with which he had been created,
but once God had imbued him with the *soul which gifted him with*

life he changed and whatever had been accomplished by the life force was now accomplished by his soul.

It is only in the second of the three options which we have just enumerated that man shares his life force with the animals. It is only in the context of that interpretation that one might reasonably fear that if he were to eat the animal's blood his faculties might be coarsened by that contact.

Clearly, then, we have the right to assume that Ramban takes this option as the operative one, perhaps because it accords with Targum's approach. In subsequent chapters we will be making good use of this discovery.

he very short time which mankind spent in the Garden of Eden is fraught with mystery. We have very little idea of how Adam perceived himself, the logic of his existence, the purpose of his life. There was neither memory nor precedent to guide him, nothing that could define his unique role among the trees and the animals which preceded him there.[1] There was a lot for him to learn.

Let us examine some of the *pesukim* in Bereishis from which we can learn how the Ribono shel Olam set about educating Adam towards life in the strange environment in which he suddenly found himself. It will take us a few chapters but with patience and application we will get there. In the meantime the careful analysis to which we will subject some of the most relevant verses will be its own reward.

After Bereishis 2:7 where we hear how God formed Adam and how He invested him with the *soul which gifted him with life,* we read as follows: *God before[2] [He brought forth all the earth's greenery] had planted a Garden in Eden and placed there the man whom He had formed.[3]*

As mentioned in note 3, we have followed Ramban's rendering of *mikedem.* Here is how he perceives what happened.

אבל ענין "ויטע ה' אלהים", להגיד שהיו **מטע** ה' , **כי טרם שגזר על הארץ "תוצא הארץ דשא" גזר במקום ההוא שיהיה שם גן**, ואמר "בכאן יהיה אילן פלוני ובכאן אילן פלוני" כערוגות המטעים, ולא היה כדרך שאר מקומות הארץ שאמר "תדשא הארץ דשא ועץ פרי", והצמיחה בלא סדר:

והנה אילני גן עדן גזר בהם לעשות ענף ולשאת פרי לעד לעולם, לא יזקין בארץ שרשם, ובעפר לא ימות גזעם, אין צריכין לעובד וזומר, שאילו היו צריכין עבודה, אחרי שגורש האדם משם מי עבד אותם. גם זה טעם "ויטע ה' אלהים", שהיו מטעיו מעשה ידיו וקיימים לעולמים, כענין שנאמר (יחזקאל מז יב) לא יבול עלהו ולא יתום פריו וכו', כי מימיו מן המקדש המה יוצאים. אם כן מה טעם "ויניחהו בגן עדן לעבדה ולשמרה" (להלן פסוק טו), שהניחו שם להיות

זורע לו חטים ומיני תבואות וכל עשב זורע זרע וערוגות הבשמים, וקוצר
ותולש ואוכל כרצונו.

Here is a paraphrase.

> On the third day of Creation, *before God called upon the
> earth to bring forth its greenery,* God decreed that a Garden be
> planted in this particular place. In contrast to the world out-
> side the Garden where trees and grasses would grow in profu-
> sion without any particular order being imposed, here there
> was careful design. God decreed that this tree should grow
> here, that one over there.
>
> Moreover, this Garden carried the imprint of the Divine
> favor with which it had come into being. The trees which
> populated this Garden were to grow and develop forever with-
> out dying or even aging. No pruning or other care would be
> required. . . . If, later, we will learn that God placed Adam in
> the Garden *to cultivate it and to guard it,* this would not refer
> to the trees. It means simply that if he would want to plant
> vegetable plots or spice beds, he would be able to do so by
> his own efforts.

I wonder how many of you, dear Readers, were as surprised as I was
when the full impact of Ramban's rendering of *mikedem* hit me.
I admit that I had never really given this matter much thought or
really any thought at all but intuitively I had always imagined that
this Garden came last. I had imagined that since the third day of
Creation the earth had been covered with trees and greenery, scattered around without any special order; and that when Adam appeared, God designed a Garden for him.

Ramban tells us that it was not so at all. He insists that we return to the morning of the third day. The world is barren. There
is not a single leaf or blade of grass anywhere. The concept "vegetation" or "greenery" still lies in the future. If there had been an
observer, he would not have had any inkling of what was to come
next. And the first thing that God does is to design a Garden and
bring it into being. Before the idea of vegetation even exists, God,

so to speak, moves far ahead of the natural, introducing a garden of serenity and beauty that cannot come about without intelligent providence.

I find myself wondering why God would have wanted to plant the Garden before he had even called upon the earth to produce anything at all. Why plant trees before the idea "tree" even existed? Why jump ahead of prudent, measured progress. Man would anyway appear only on the sixth day. Why have the Garden sitting there with nobody to enjoy its peace?

In the following chapter we will learn from Radak that the essential quality of this Garden was the perfect balance between an outer, this-worldly attractiveness and an inner Presence, a balance which meant that life lived there would partake of as close a proximity to the Divine as is given humans to experience.[4] Almost by definition, that balance determined that the physical was to be subordinated to the spiritual. If any proof were needed that this was indeed the hierarchy which obtained there, it is made clear in Bereishis 2:16 and 17, which read, *God commanded man, saying, "You may eat from every tree of the garden. But from the tree of Knowledge of Good and Evil do not eat. . . . "* Apparently, God's command was required not only to forbid eating from the prohibited Tree of Knowledge but also to grant permission to partake of the trees which were to be permitted. Enjoyment of the pleasant life in Eden is legitimized solely from the fact that it is an expression of God's will.

This would be the perfect setting for man. The Ribono shel Olam conceived man himself to have a similar balance: the earthly components within man would be subordinated to the Godly as the possessive *lamed* which we examined in the previous chapter makes clear.

On the third day of Creation, when God was ready to clothe the naked earth He directed His attention to Gan Eden before anything else. It was there, and nowhere else, that the drama of the kiss between heaven and earth was to play itself out. The wild, unplanned jungle that was to lie beyond the confines of the Garden would serve only *de facto* man. The jungle reflected the untamed life that had rebelled against its subordinate state. The feral vegetation was suited to serve man who had been untrue to his mission and frustrated God's intention. That Gan Eden did not spread all over the globe was, as it were, God's admission that provision had to be made for a "B" plan.

We will think more about these issues in the coming chapters.

*W*e began the previous chapter with the remark that Adam must have had a lot to learn when God first placed him in Gan Eden. There were no role models to whom he could look, no memories upon which he might draw, no basis at all, at least as far as we can see from the story as it is told to us, for reaching any conclusions about what he was and what he was expected to do. There was really nobody to help him except the Ribono shel Olam Himself. He would know what the Ribono shel Olam would choose to reveal to him and as for the rest, he would have to work it out for himself.

Here is what happened. *Now God commanded the man, saying, "Eat freely from all the trees in the Garden. However, do not eat from the Tree of Knowledge . . . for on the day that you eat from it you will surely die."* That is all.[1] Not one word concerning any duties of the heart,[2] nor any encouragement to make use of the close proximity of God to strive for goodness and sanctity.[3]

The only way in which I can understand why the Ribono shel Olam would have kept silent concerning this all-important aspect of Adam's life is on the basis of the conclusions which we reached in the last few chapters. God created Adam specifically so that the heavenly and the earthly elements of his personality relate to each other precisely. The *soul which gifted him with life* defined his essence; the animal-like life force was totally subordinate to it. There had as yet been no slippage, there was no thought of desiring anything other than the fulfillment of the soul's natural craving for closeness to God. Striving for goodness and sanctity was as natural to Adam as breathing. No exhortations were required. If there was a need to teach Adam anything at all, it was how to handle his physical desires, those cravings prompted by the healthy but as yet not independently functioning earthly component. We could, for example, imagine that his intuitive sense would have led him to favor some form of asceticism or unnatural abstinence. Immediately upon his entry into Gan Eden, the Ribono shel Olam disabused him of any such ideas. Here is how.

Much depends on how we understand the *command*[4] in the verse which we quoted at the beginning of this essay. Does the *command* apply to only the second part of God's exhortation, that he would not be permitted to eat from the Tree of Knowledge, or is the first part, *Eat freely from all the trees of the Garden*, also a part of the *command*?

At first, Radak inclines towards the first option. How, he reasons, can we be *commanded* to "eat freely"? However, in the end he retreats from this position. He concludes that we are *commanded* to enjoy whichever of the earth's bounties are permitted to us.

This was Adam's first lesson. "Do not be afraid of this delightful world in which I have placed you. Its variegated offerings of taste, texture and color are not there to trap you into a betrayal of the spark of divinity with which I have endowed you. I placed you in the Garden so that you might be happy and learn to appreciate how much I care for you.[5] It is your duty to take pleasure in the riches which I have placed at your disposal!"

All this sounds strange. Mesilas Yesharim teaches that "*perishus*," abstinence, is a constituent part of "*chasidus*," piety. Permission to eat is one thing; a command to indulge is quite another.

Let us try to understand.

Here is how Radak describes God's purpose in bringing Adam to Gan Eden.

אלא הביאו לגן עדן, שיהיה שם ויתעדן מפרותיו בלא עמל בנגלה, ובנסתר לנפשו.

God brought him to the Garden of Eden so that he might luxuriate in its fruits without it costing him any effort. This was on the open, physical level. At a hidden [more spiritual] level he was there for the benefit of his soul.

This Radak is of great interest because he postulates a hidden, spiritual dimension. To the best of my knowledge, there is no indication for this in the text. Apparently, as we suggested above, given

Adam's perfection as the product of God's own handiwork, this spiritual aspect of life in the Garden is self-evident.

Whatever is the source for Radak, he clearly postulates that life in Gan Eden was made up of two extremes. One cannot help thinking that these two dimensions would make uncomfortable neighbors. It is certainly not obvious to us how close proximity to the Ribono shel Olam comports with an apparent centralizing of sybaritic indulgence.[6] Was, then, life in the Garden riven with tension between the two poles? Did Adam feel guilty when he plucked a fruit from one of the permitted trees and enjoyed it?

Our discomfort with the unexpected duality which apparently punctuated life in the Garden stems from our "post-Eden and pre-Messiah" mentality. Most of us feel some degree of guilt about the physical indulgences which we permit ourselves. Such self-flagellation was meaningless in the ideal world which the Ribono shel Olam had planned for us. We may assume that Adam ate the fruit with relish and without any inner conflict.

Let us for just a moment turn to Malachi's picture of the *Yemos HaMoshiach*, the Messianic age: *The sun will shine for those of you who stand in awe of me. It will be a benevolent sun carrying healing in its rays. Then you will go out and become fat like stall-fed calves* (Malachi 3:20).

Can we trust our eyes? Is this really what makes us anticipate Moshiach with so much longing? Does it not sound a little crass? Do we *really* want to look like stall-fed calves? Clearly the prophet is educating us into realizing that in essence there is no contradiction at all between an all-consuming love of God and an enjoyment of the largess which He has showered upon us with such an open hand. We experience physical pleasures as an illicit indulgence because we are held captive by an unruly earth component (see previous chapter) which has broken loose from the thrall of the *soul which gifted him with life* and has reverted to an animal-like focus upon the body as an end in itself. However, in Messianic times we will function as we were meant to function. Though the sun appears as a symbol of this-worldly pampering[7] throughout TaNaCh, at that time it will become "benevolent."[8] Far from inveigling us into improper lust for gratification, the sun will heal us from the imbalance that has often made us into ill-functioning invalids.

In Gan Eden, the marriage between Radak's *open* and *hidden* pleasures is a happy, conflict-free union.

*I*n the previous chapter we had the Ribono shel Olam telling Adam, "I placed you in the Garden so that you might be happy and learn to appreciate how much I care for you." The time has come to give this assertion some body and then to go on from there to see where all this may lead us.

Bereishis 2:15 reads as follows: *HaShem, God, took the man and placed him in the Garden of Eden to cultivate it and to guard it.* Here are Radak's remarks.

ופירוש "ויקח" "וינחהו" שלקחו ממקום שנברא שם, סמוך לגן עדן, והנחהו
בגן עדן. ולמה לא יצרו תחלה בגן עדן אחר שהיה סופו להניחו שם? כדי
שיהיה המקום ההוא חביב עליו יותר, שהיה חדש אצלו, ושיכיר כי האל הולך
ומטיב עמו.

The words *"He took"* and *"He placed him"* imply that he took him from a different place, one that lay in the vicinity of Gan Eden, and placed him in Gan Eden. Now, why, since he was anyway destined to live in the Garden, was he not created there? It was in order that he would appreciate the Garden the more because it was new for him. God wanted him to realize that his Creator was constantly out for his good.

It is a remarkable passage, is it not? The very first lesson which Adam was to learn was that he was loved and that the Ribono shel Olam cared about his welfare. We cannot even begin to fathom the loneliness which Adam must have felt when he came to his senses in the wild jungle outside Eden. Where was he? What was he to do? What was his place among the tangle which surrounded him. In the middle of his confusion, God, so to speak, took him by the hand and led him into a gorgeous garden—every tree thoughtfully placed, every shrub becomingly arranged; all this for him. Somebody had thought about him, Someone had anticipated his longing for order and serenity. Adam learned very quickly that he was not entirely alone.

There was still another important lesson that his experience had taught him. He would constantly be reminded that life in the Garden could not be taken for granted.[1] The path along which the Ribono shel Olam had brought him to Gan Eden pointed in both directions. If it served as a way in, it could also serve as a way out. If it could be given it could also be withheld. It was important that he should realize this.

God had as much as told him this immediately after He had created him. Let us remember that this took place *outside* the Garden. Here is what Bereishis 1:28 tells us: *God blessed them and said to them, "Be fruitful and multiply; fill the earth and subdue it."* Now who are the people through whom the earth is to be filled? Very clearly, had Adam not sinned he would have remained in the Garden forever. We must conclude, and so must Adam have concluded, that the Garden had to be earned and that there would always be people who would not make the grade.

This, of course, brings us face-to-face with a problem. If one must earn Gan Eden, why did God permit Adam to enter without testing him in any way?

Here is what appears to me to be the solution. In chapter 5 we demonstrated that Ramban favors the explanation that the *lamed* of *l'nefesh chayah* is a preposition denoting possession. I quote: "Once man had been imbued with the *soul which gifted him with life*, the earlier life force became subordinate to this soul, became in a real sense possessed by it. Man is not to be made up of two equal faculties, the one material, the other from heaven. The soul is always to preponderate." That is what God wanted and that is how God made Adam. This first man, at the moment of his creation before he had had a chance to err, measured up completely to the ideal which God had had in mind, and his natural environment was Gan Eden, where the balance between the Radak's open and hidden gifts precisely mirrored the balance of his person.[2] There was no question of any merit being required since Adam, as he was at that heady moment, was exactly as he should be.

When Adam sinned, the earth component in him slipped its

leash and took on a life of its own. With the balance disturbed, he became an unwelcome intruder within the rarefied perfection of Gan Eden. Henceforth, both he and the children to whom he would pass on his deficiencies would have to undertake correctives which would once more permit them access to the Garden. Pending those correctives, they would all have to make do on the outside, where the chaos which they would meet while fighting thorn and thistle would reflect the inner chaos brought on by a brash, hard-to-control, animal-like life force. We all know that the way back is not an easy one.

e are close to the end of our trip. We have been to a lot of places, seen a lot of sights. I feel fairly confident that we have understood Ramban's position correctly. He stands with Targum that Adam was alive, though less than human, before God imbued him with the *nishmas chaim*. Even after he became human, the basic life force remained as it had been before, a product of the earth as was the life force of the animals. In his case, however, it was now to be totally subordinated to his humanity. Adam's rights to Gan Eden were to be conditioned by the degree to which he would maintain this subordinate relationship. He was exiled when the life force asserted an independence to which it could lay no claim. We are still trying to make our way back.

We will make one final stop before we return to the question which we left unanswered in chapter 1. We will observe the drama in which Adam comes to the realization that he must find a sympathetic partner to walk with him through life.

Before embarking on this final adventure, I reread the opening paragraph of this essay. I certainly stand by what is written there. Still I do not like it. I have taken a human dilemma and drained it of its humanity. I have dealt with our very essence and treated it as a problem in mechanics. There is a certain amount of this, a certain amount of the other; the interaction between the various parts is to take place in such and such a manner. Balance is good, imbalance is bad and so on.

What we should really have asked ourselves is how Adam Ha-Rishon *felt* about himself. Did the disparate elements within him cause him unease? Did he wonder who he was? It seems likely that he did. Let us recall that for all we know, Adam had a memory of the time when he had been a subhuman, unblessed with the gift of speech, no different from any of the animals who might have crossed his path. At that time, he would have identified himself with these, probably ranking high in the hierarchy but, nevertheless, of a piece with them. Suddenly he undergoes a metamorphosis. His body has not changed in any way. If, let us say, he was hungry before, he would still have been hungry now, but something had suddenly become very different. Where before his mind had only been marked by the most primitive impressions: color, smell, texture, sound, pain, temperature and so on, he was suddenly capable of the most sublime thoughts and had become master of a complex language through which he could express the deepest secrets of a heart suddenly turned sensitive to the gamut of human emotions.

Did he brood about what he was to make of himself now? Were the changes of which he had become aware quantitative or qualitative? Could he still hope for companionship within the animal world or was he now utterly alone?

Let us study the story of the creation of Chavah and see where it will take us. We begin with Bereishis 2:18.

ויאמר יקוק אלהים **לא טוב** היות האדם לבדו אעשה לו עזר כנגדו.

God said, "It is not good for man to be alone. I will make him a helper who will be compatible with him."

I have discussed this *pasuk* at length in my book *Beginnings.* What I wrote there remains relevant here, at least as far as this opening verse is concerned. Here is an excerpt from chapter 5 of that book:

Ramban begins with the assumption that there was never any thought that Adam would not have children. He was part of the physical world and the faculty of reproduction is a hallmark of physicality. However, there was always the possibility of having both the male and female procreative components built into one person as they are in certain forms of plant and animal life. These would interact with one another without Adam's volition. God's . . . לא טוב marks the decision to create a discrete marriage partner for Adam.

Here is how Ramban puts it.

. . . וראה הקב"ה כי טוב שיהיה העזר עומד לנגדו, והוא יראנו, ויפרד ממנו
ויתחבר אליו כפי רצונו (בראשית ב י"ח).

God thought it best that the *ezer* be a separate person, one
whom he could see. Moreover the decision to either withdraw
from or join with this *ezer* would be Adam's (Bereishis 2:18).

Why? Why did this system appear to God to be the better one?

It seems to me that God's decision could be phrased in the following way. The interaction between male and female organs in
those life forms that contain both may well be a highly efficient
method for managing reproduction. However, whatever else is involved, *ahavah*[1] is not. God wanted the children of Adam to be
children born of *ahavah*.

Ramban confirms this idea. At the end of this passage, the Torah
tells us, *Because of all this, man will leave his father and his mother
and cleave to his wife with whom he has become one and the same
flesh.* Ramban has this to say:

והנכון בעיני, כי הבהמה והחיה אין להם דבקות בנקבותיהן, אבל יבא הזכר על
איזה נקבה שימצא, וילכו להם, ומפני זה אמר הכתוב, בעבור שנקבת האדם
היתה עצם מעצמיו ובשר מבשרו, ודבק בה, והיתה בחיקו כבשרו, ויחפוץ בה
להיותה תמיד עמו. וכאשר היה זה באדם, הושם טבעו בתולדותיו, להיות
הזכרים מהם דבקים בנשותיהם, עוזבים את אביהם ואת אמם, ורואים את
נשותיהן כאלו הן עמם לבשר אחד.

To my mind the following is the correct way to understand
this phrase. Besides a few species of mammals, most animals
do not form lasting partnerships. They join with any available partner and then walk away. Humans are different. Because the woman was born, bone from Adam's bone and flesh
from his flesh, he felt at one with her, achieving total union
with her as she lies in his embrace. Because of this he craves
her constant companionship. This attitude was passed on to
all of Adam's descendants. They all wish to be one with their
wives and leave their parents' home in order to establish their
own families.

Ramban does not make the following point, but it seems to me to be a legitimate thought. I feel that the reason that the Ribono shel Olam first created Adam as an androgynous being, an efficient child-producing mechanism without even a hint of the warming *ahavah* which accompanies the joining of husband and wife, and only then provided him with a "compatible helper," is similar to the reason that He created Adam outside Gan Eden and only then brought him into the Garden. In the previous chapter we learned from Radak that this was done *in order that he would appreciate the garden the more because it was new for him. God wanted him to realize that his Creator was constantly out for his good.* The parallelism is clear. By first endowing Adam with both the male and female elements, the Ribono shel Olam was laying the groundwork for the unbounded joy and appreciation which Adam would feel when he would wake from his slumber and set eyes upon the woman who would be his life's partner.

Very well. The stage has been set for the creation of Chavah and we would not have been at all surprised if the next verse would have described how this took place. If verse 21 (*God then made the man fall into a deep state of unconsciousness . . .*) would have followed hard upon our verse 18, we would not have been in any way troubled.

But it does not. We first have an account of a seemingly unconnected incident. God brings all living creatures to Adam, charging him to assign a name to each one. Quite apart from the difficulty in grasping what precisely took place, we are hard put to understand its relevance to the appearance of Chavah.

Rashi, indeed, sees only an indirect connection. The actual assigning of names had no inherent bearing upon the search for a wife. It was only that while the animals were in front of him to be named, Adam observed the males and females coupling with one another and became acutely aware of his own incompleteness.

We will see that Ramban differs. The story of the naming *is* the story of the search for a compatible companion.

At this point we must study verses 19 and 20:

יט. ויצר יקוק אלהים מן האדמה כל חית השדה ואת כל עוף השמים ויבא אל האדם לראות מה יקרא לו וכל אשר יקרא לו האדם נפש חיה הוא שמו:

כ. ויקרא האדם שמות לכל הבהמה ולעוף השמים ולכל חית השדה ולאדם
לא מצא עזר כנגדו:

19. Now God had formed all the undomesticated animals and all the birds from the earth and [now] brought them to the man[2] to see what he would call them. Whichever of these animals man would call *nefesh chayah* that would be its name.

20. Then the man assigned names to all the domesticated animals, to all the birds of heaven and to all the undomesticated animals. But for Adam he did not find a helpmeet who would be compatible with him.

Let us first take care of some housekeeping problems and then we will try to understand what happened. Before anything else I ask you to note that I left *nefesh chayah* untranslated. This is because it is particularly difficult to accommodate in this particular context.

The problem is that the verb *kara,*[3] when used in the sense *to give a name*, is transitive and therefore requires an object. The simplest translation of the relevant phrase would therefore be, *Whatever creature man would call by the [specific] name* NEFESH CHAYAH *that would be its name.* Rashi had great problems with this translation. Every one in the animal world was a *nefesh chayah*, a living being. How would *nefesh chayah* be an appropriate name for any single one of the creatures?

Because of this, Rashi felt the need to invert the words of the verse and to read it as though instead of *kol asher yikra lo ha'adam nefesh chayah hu shemo,* it were written: *Kol nefesh chayah asher yikra lo ha'adam [shem] hu shemo.*[4]

Ramban is able to do without any inversion because he views the whole story from an entirely different perspective. In his view, the Ribono shel Olam was forcing Adam into the realization that he would not be able to find a suitable partner from within the animal world. Here is how: The names which Adam was to assign were not "names" at all in the conventional sense. Rather, he was called upon to divide the animals into groupings ("names" in the sense of isolating and identifying salient features) which enabled the various species within that grouping to procreate with one another.

42

The *helper* whom Adam needed was one with whom he would be able to bring forth children.

Here is what Ramban says, together with a paraphrase:

ויתכן שיהיה פירושו בענין העזר, והכוונה לומר כי האדם נפש חיה, כמו שאמר ויהי האדם לנפש חיה (לעיל ב ז), וכמו שפירשתי, והביא לפניו המינין כולן, וכל מין מהם שיקראנו האדם בשמו, ויאמר בו שהוא נפש חיה כמותו, הוא יהיה שמו, ויהיה לו לעזר כנגדו. והוא קרא לכולן ולא מצא לעצמו עזר שיקרא לו "נפש חיה" כשמו.

It is possible to look upon Adam's "naming" of the animals as part of his search for a partner with whom he would be able to have children. Now man was a unique form of *nefesh chayah*[5] and therefore needed to identify a kindred *nefesh chayah*. This is what he needed and this is what he could not find.

Accordingly, the verse is to be understood as follows: *To whomever the man will attach the name* NEFESH CHAYAH *[in the sense that this description applies to himself], that would determine its category and mark it as being of a kind through which he could bring forth children.*

So, the search is on. The animals all pass in front of Adam, he contemplates their nature and divides them into appropriate groupings. The expectation, at least from Adam's point of view, is that from within this world he would be able to find a partner.

Here is how Ramban explains what might have happened had the experiment worked out.

והענין, כי הקב"ה הביא כל חית השדה וכל עוף השמים לפני אדם, והוא הכיר טבעם וקרא להם שמות, כלומר השם הראוי להם כפי טבעיהם. ובשמות נתבאר הראוי להיות עזר לחבירו, כלומר הראוים להוליד זה מזה. ואפילו אם נאמין בשמות שהם בהסכמה, לא טבעיות (מו"נ ב ל), נאמר שקריאת השמות היא הבדלת המינים, כי עברו לפניו זכר ונקבה והתבונן בטבעם, איזה מהם עזר לחבירו, כלומר המוליד ממנו, והודיע זה בשמות, כי בהבהמה הדקה קרא בשם אחר, שכולן עזר זה לזה בתולדה שיולידו זה מזה, והגסה בשם אחר, והחיה בשם אחר, שלא יולידו מין זה מזה, וכן כולן. ולא מצא בכולן שתהיה בטבעה עזר לו ותקרא בשמו, כי קריאת השמות היא הבדלת המינים והפרד כחותם זה מזה, כאשר פירשתי למעלה.

ואין הענין שיהיה ביד האדם למצא בהם עזר לו, כי בטבעם נבראו, אבל
שאם יראה טבעו נאות באחד המינים ויבחר בו, היה הקב"ה מתקן טבעו אליו
כאשר עשה בצלע, ולא יצטרך לבנותו בנין חדש.

This is what happened: God brought all the animals and birds
to Adam who was able to discern their nature and thereby
to classify them. These classifications are the "names" which
Adam gave them and their effect was to group animals which
were able to procreate together in discrete classes. Thus the
smaller animals constituted one grouping, the larger animals
and the undomesticated animals each, another grouping.

However, Adam did not find a single one among the animals which shared his nature to the extent that they could be
said to belong in a single grouping (to carry the same "name").
Now it must be understood that no animal *as it was* could ever
have suited Adam as a partner. The animals were endowed
with all the properties that their nature demanded and would
have been physically unsuited to couple with Adam. The exercise was meant only to determine whether there was among
them one to whom Adam felt attracted. Had such a one been
found God would have formed an appropriate partner for
Adam from that animal instead of taking a part of Adam's
own body to form the woman.

It is a strange story, is it not? I think that all of us feel a kind of re-
vulsion at the idea that Adam might have believed that he would
be able to find his life's partner from among the animals. However,
we must remember that since we live in a world in which the human race is comprised of men and women, we find it hard to imagine any other model. Moreover, none of us shares Adam's history
of having once, quite literally, belonged within the animal world.
If, in our imagination, we could transport ourselves into the unrelieved, unimaginable loneliness which Adam must have felt, we
would be more understanding of his anxious longing.

What was the point of the whole exercise?[6]

It seems to me (though not necessarily according to Ramban)
that the Ribono shel Olam put Adam through this experience in
order to impress upon him how thoroughly his brutish life force,

the one which, as we saw above in chapter 5, he shared with the animals, had, in fact, changed by being subordinated to the *nish-mas chaim*. Although at a purely physical level there was much that he had in common with the beasts, there was no longer any commonality among him and them. Adam needed to learn the secret of sublimation. He needed to realize that he was not, and need never be, a prisoner of his brutish past.

He also needed to learn that the chasm which separated him from the beasts was not unbridgeable. Let him but be careless of his spiritual riches, let him allow his animal-like *life force* to assert independence, and he will discover a snarling beast within himself, difficult to control, next to impossible to defang and lure back to its nonthreatening dependency.

We have come a long way since chapter 1. We are just about ready to attempt an answer to the question which we raised there. That answer deserves a chapter of its own.

*T*he time has come to get back to the question which we left unanswered in chapter 1. It *does* sound like a major problem, does it not? God promises us (Devarim 30:6) a miraculous "circumcision of the heart," to take place when we will all have returned to Eretz Yisrael from our far-flung exiles. He will excise all unworthy longings and make us all naturally good. Mankind will have returned to "Eden," to the perfection of Adam before he sinned, and life will be lived by all of us as God had originally intended that it should be lived.

We cannot really imagine what exactly lies in store for us. We are so poor, so flawed, so shackled. We are so aware of our gargantuan failings, our petty silliness and our depressing smallness. The idea that a Divine "surgery" will be able to free us from the burden of simply being ourselves is hard to assimilate. Miracles are, by definition, outside our experience. We can believe, but we cannot go much further than that.

As if all this were not difficult enough, we have to come to grips with Devarim 10:16: *You are to circumcise the* ORLAH *of your hearts.* Here we, not the Ribono shel Olam, are to perform the surgery. Does this circumcision also presage a return to Eden? What precisely are we expected to do? Are we who constantly fail in our simplest duties expected to find our own way back to perfection?

This was our question and the time has come to tackle it. For simplicity's sake we will refer to the two passages by the names of the *parashah* in which they occur. The passage from Devarim 30:6 is in Nitzavim, the one from Devarim 10:16 is from Eikev.

I believe that we will find the answer in a subtle change in the wording of the two passages. Those of you who do not enjoy careful textual dissections are going to have to bear with me for a few moments. Do not feel threatened. It is all really quite simple.

Here are the two phrases:

NITZAVIM/נצבים	EIKEV/עקב
... ומל ה' אלהיך את לבבך	... ומלתם את **ערלת** לבבכם
HaShem your God will circumcise your heart...	You shall circumcise the *orlah* of your hearts...

The Nitzavim passage speaks of God circumcising our hearts (not the *orlah* of our hearts). The Eikev passage uses *orlah*. Let us see whether we can work out the difference.

Ramban to Bereishis 17:14 will help.

ולפי דעתי הדבר מפורש בכתוב, כי לא אמר "ונמלתם את ערלתכם" שיהיה
הדבר בספק, וכן לא אמר "ערלת בשרכם" כמו שיאמר ערלת לבבכם (דברים
י טז) וערלת שפתים (עיי' שמות ו יב). אבל אמר "בשר ערלתכם", שתכרתו
הבשר שהוא ערלה בכם, כלומר הבשר האוטם בכם, ואין בגוף בשר אוטם
וכוסה אבר שיכרת הבשר ההוא וישאר בלא ערלה זולתי בשר החופה את
העטרה שהזכירו חכמים. (שבת קלז א)

Here is the background to what Ramban is saying: When God commanded Avraham to circumcise himself, He used, *unemaltem es b'sar orlaschem, you shall cut off the flesh of your* "ORLAH." What exactly does this mean? The word "*orlah*" occurs in all kinds of contexts[1] and can convey all sorts of ideas. Commentators struggle to explain how these words yield the particular process which we know as circumcision.

Ramban maintains that a careful analysis of the text yields the meaning explicitly. He suggests that the word *orlah* can be used both literally, the actual foreskin, and metaphorically to describe any impediment to normal use. For example, when Moshe Rabbeinu describes himself as a stutterer by using *aral sefasayim*, he did not mean to imply that there was any physical block to his speech but simply that it was not as clear as it should have been.

Ramban formulated a rule which will enable us to determine when *orlah* is used literally and when metaphorically. To understand this rule, we have to make a short excursus into the arcane world of Hebrew grammar. I promise that it will be short and painless.

The genitive (possessive voice) is known in Hebrew grammar as the *semichus*, "bringing close" form. It brings two simple words into proximity with each other[2] in order to create a new complex idea, one that expresses possession. Here is an example which we all know: *Banim* in its simple, unconnected form means children or sons. However, when it becomes a *nismach*,[3] that which is brought close, to a *somech*, that which brings it close, it gets shortened into *benei*. Thus we have BENEI *Yisrael*, rather than *Banim shel Yisrael*. In this example, "*Yisrael*" is the *somech*, and "*Benei*," the *nismach*.

For practical purposes, we can state Ramban's rule as follows: *orlah*, or one of its forms, as *somech*, is literal; *orlah* as *nismach* is metaphorical. Thus, *b'sar orloso* (*orlah* as *somech*) is *the flesh of the* FORESKIN (literal); *aral sefasayim* (*orlah* as *nismach*) is one *who stutters* (metaphorical).

The theory might be stated as follows: in the *semichus* form, the *somech* preponderates; it is the subject to which the *nismach* is subordinate. For example, in *aral sefasayim*, it is the *somech*, *sefsayim*, lips, which determines the meaning of *aral*. We know what lips are, so *aral* will have to mean, *an* ORLAH *to the extent that lips can have a "blockage."* Since clearly there is no physical barrier to which lips are subject, the meaning must be metaphorical. Hence, *aral* in this combination stands for whatever cause there is for stuttering.

However, in *besar orloso*, *orlah* is the *somech* and accordingly the determinant. We know what *orlah* means; it is a physical blockage, that is, the foreskin. The *basar*, flesh, of this *orlah* can only refer to the one place on the body at which flesh does indeed "stop up" an organ. We know precisely what this means.

We are now ready to go back to the question which precipitated this whole discussion. We wondered how the Eikev passage could charge us with circumcising our heart when, as the Nitzavim passage makes clear, the circumcision of the heart is a miracle to be performed by God Himself at the end of days.

Let us remember the difference in the wording of the two passages. The Nitzavim passage has "your heart" as the direct object of *u'mal*, while Eikev has "the ORLAH of your heart" as the direct object of *umaltem*. Conscious of Ramban's rule that where *orlah* is a *nismach* we should expect a metaphorical use, we conclude that in the Eikev passage we are not talking of an actual blockage. Rather, the *orlas halev* mentioned there is akin to the *orlas sefasayim* of Moshe Rabbeinu. It is something which impedes the normal functioning of lips or, in this case, heart, without being a physical stoppage.

Because of this Ramban there defines this command as follows: *That your heart will be hospitable to the perception of truth.*[4] Now, we all know how distorting our predilections can be and that it is difficult to muster honest objectivity. Still, if we do manage it, we can hardly be said to have accomplished the miraculous. A love of truth, a stout heart and a dash of courage and the thing is done.

By contrast, Nitzavim speaks of *circumcising the heart* itself. There is a blockage to the heart which must be removed in order to partake of the Messianic age. Now, while it is clear that there is no physical obstruction which requires removal, there is apparently a spiritual entity which rises to the level of a "stoppage" in that context.

Ramban to the Nitzavim passage explains exactly what this is.

אבל לימות המשיח, תהיה הבחירה בטוב להם טבע, לא יתאוה להם הלב למה שאינו ראוי ולא יחפוץ בו כלל. והיא המילה הנזכרת כאן. **כי החמדה והתאוה ערלה ללב, ומול הלב הוא שלא יחמוד ולא יתאוה.** וישוב האדם בזמן ההוא לאשר היה קודם חטאו של אדם הראשון, שהיה עושה מה שראוי לעשות ולא היה לו ברצונו דבר והפכו, כמו שפירשתי בסדר בראשית (ב ט):

Here is a paraphrase:

Chemdah and *ta'avah*, the desire and craving for illicit pleasures, are the *orlah*, the blockage of the heart. They divert the natural longing for goodness and purity to the ignoble and the shameful. The promise that God will circumcise our hearts is a promise that these blockages will be "cut away."

Once Moshiach will have come, it will be natural for people to choose good over bad. It will not be a matter of struggling with one's baser self, because we, having returned to the perfect balance which obtained when Adam was created, will simply not desire anything that is in opposition to God's will.

The Nitzavim passage does indeed predict a miraculous turn in human affairs. We will at last come face-to-face with our real selves. For the first time in our post-Eden history we will be truly free. The changing of our very nature cannot be accomplished by anybody but the Ribono shel Olam Himself.

Eikev, it is true, demands a serious effort from us. To become receptive to pure, unadulterated truth in our present state is no small matter. But, withal, it is something which we can accomplish on our own.

It seems to me that we have found the correct answer to the question which we posed so many chapters ago. We have discovered it in a careful analysis of the language which the Torah uses in the two passages. What, then, was the purpose of all the intervening chapters in which we worked so hard to understand the Ramban's ideas concerning the creation of man?

I believe that the conclusions which we reached in those chapters can make a real contribution towards understanding the use of the concept "circumcision of the heart" to describe the process by which the Ribono shel Olam will reestablish the balance which was lost when Adam sinned.

From the Ramban which we just quoted, we learn that *chemdah* and *ta'avah*, desire and craving, are the *orlah* of the heart which the Ribono shel Olam is going to cut away. From our discussions in the earlier chapters we recognize these two as the illegitimate expression of the animal *life force* which, as we described it, slipped the leash of its subordination to the *nishmas chaim* and struck out on its own.

The *milas halev* of which Nitzavim speaks will be the downgrading of this lawless expansion, the lopping off of those appetites which should never have been given free rein.

PART II.
RAMBAN
ON
THE NATURE
OF
HASHGACHAH

11: INTIMATIONS
OF A VERY SPECIAL RELATIONSHIP
in which we embark upon our next sugia:
Ramban's ideas concerning
God's providence, hashgachah

You pick up a book that purports to discuss Ramban's ideas, and you feel that you will be transported back to the early Middle Ages. You do not expect any direct help in unraveling today's headlines. You recognize that his writings, particularly his commentary on Chumash, are one of the most significant repositories of Jewish *hashkafah*. At the same time you realize th at his world was not ours and the problems which beset the Jews of Gerona and Barcelona in the thirteenth century were different from those which bedevil us in our benighted generation. To bolster an appreciation for the *theories* of Judaism, he has no peer. For practical guidance you will look elsewhere.

In the section which follows, I plan to turn these perceptions on their head.

When the State of Israel was founded in 1948, I was a Yeshiva Bachur in Gateshead, with my head more in the Gemara than in what was happening in the wide world beyond. I do not recall that this epochal event made a particularly strong impression upon me at the time. I say this neither with pride nor in shame. That is just the way things were in those tumultuous postwar years. We were told, I believe with full justification, that if there were to be a rebirth of Torah after the dreadful war years and the millions whom we had lost, it would depend upon us—our seriousness, our commitment and our application. We looked upon ourselves as pioneers of Torah learning in a world which had very little understanding or sympathy for what we were doing. We were young, we were perhaps a shade too sure of ourselves, but we meant well. History, I think, will look kindly upon our exertions.

June 1967 was something else. Different people, I am sure, experienced those emotionally packed few days in different ways. For me, the dreadful fears, the constant worry, the imperfectly suppressed thoughts of the unthinkable, came wrapped in a feeling of indescribable exhilaration. Tehilim came alive for me. Again and again Dovid HaMelech reminds us that battles against us, His people, are battles against the Ribono shel Olam Himself. *Why are the nations in such a ferment? Why are they laying such ultimately useless plots? . . . It is against HaShem [that they will move. Against Him] and against His anointed one* (a paraphrase of Tehilim 2:1–2). For once, terribly but graphically, the identity of purpose and being between the Ribono shel Olam and ourselves came alive for me. Never before in our exile had we been granted a vision of the Ribono shel Olam as *Ish Milchamah*, a mighty warrior, unsheathing His sword in defense of everything good and pure and holy. And it was we, in all our weakness and failings, who stood with Him and were one with Him. Those were heady days.

Still even 1967 is almost forty years ago and for the under-fifties crowd it is hardly even a hazy memory.

So we leapfrog to 1990 and the Gulf War which is still alive in the memories of most of us. It is where I want to get for the purpose of this section. Here is why. I recently came across a booklet which was published in the wake of that war by the Bais Yaakov of Benei Berak. Its purpose was to encourage people to think seriously about what had happened and, more particularly, about what did not happen. I was struck by an article by Rabbi Nathan Kohn, parts of which I want to share with you.

Here is a paraphrase:

> . . . We had no idea at all of the real and palpable danger in which we stood. For years Saddam Hussein had built up a fearsome arsenal for the express purpose of destroying us. The fire power which he had amassed defies description or quantification. The Ribono shel Olam frustrated his purpose but showed us clearly to what we had been exposed.
>
> Here is how. On the last day of the war, a Scud Missile fell on an American military post, killing a large number of soldiers and wounding many others. Suddenly we realized from what we had been saved in our holy land. Thirty-nine Scuds and only one injury! The international press refused to credit

that this is what actually happened. They were sure that the censor was at work to hide the truth. But we do know the truth. God made sure that we should recognize the extent of our salvation. After what happened, we would never be able to tell ourselves that there had never really been anything much to fear.

Let us consider further that the Ribono shel Olam did not permit this tragedy to happen until the very last day of the war. Who can tell what panic would have ensued among us had we known the awesome power of these missiles while they were still raining down upon us. Think of the dreadful fears which we were spared.

We did not have to lift a finger in our own defense. Our battles were fought by others. Think of the thousands of sacrifices which we did not have to bring in fighting such a mighty army.

Think further. Who made sure that we did not have to go out to fight? Of course it was the Americans. Why were they so eager that we should not be involved? Of course it was their coalition partners, Egypt and Saudi Arabia, who refused to stand shoulder to shoulder with Jews in a war against their Arab brother. Our most bitter and bloodthirsty enemies were the ones who made sure that we should not spill a drop of blood. Is it not reminiscent of Pharaoh who, after killing thousands so that the savior of Israel should not live, ended up by rearing him in his own palace?

I found this to be a particularly strong presentation. I do not think that any reader of this book will have any quarrel with Rabbi Kohn's assertion that the workings of a very open Divine providence can be clearly apprehended here. I believe that inasmuch as most of us have actually experienced these miraculous events, at least by proxy, they serve as a perfect springboard for a discussion of Ramban's teachings concerning *hashgachah*. It is to the examination of this profound issue that we will devote the next few chapters.

12: A VULTURE'S LOVE

*T*orah is a stern mistress. *Everything* that we learn demands our enthusiastic interest. *He who declares that he is attracted to one* sugia *more than to another will never truly possess the Torah* (Eiruvin 64a). We learn not because our intellectual taste buds are stimulated but because the Ribono shel Olam wishes us to know and love and live His Torah.

Still, I am pretty sure that, perhaps surreptitiously, most of us are attracted to a particular *pasuk* or *parashah* more than to another. Construed strictly, the Eiruvin passage may even wink at such weakness. Its stricture against playing favorites may be limited to *Torah shebe'al peh*. It uses *shemu'ah*, received wisdom, and that certainly indicates some halachic disquisition. So, perhaps we secret sinners are after all on safe ground.

I am always particularly moved by Devarim 32:10, *Like a vulture[1] arousing its chicks,[2] hovering over its young. Spreading its wings he picks them up so that he may carry them on his pinions.* As a metaphor for the love and caring which the Ribono shel Olam lavishes upon us, it is peerless. The mighty wings are held in check, reduced to a flutter so as not to frighten the little ones.[3] Then the chicks are positioned for the flight where they are most comfortable and can feel most protected and loved. Mother[4] is close by. There is no warmer or more delicious feeling in the world.

I was sitting at my desk, allowing my imagination to transport me to the crags and outcroppings of the mighty mountains where this drama plays itself out.[5] As I watched, this scene seemed to fade away and was replaced by snarling dogs, the whip, the club, the flames and the horrors which so often were the props which littered the stage of Jewish experience. I found myself wondering which one of these images was the truer picture of our trek through history. Gradually this question, as all good questions tend to do, dissolved itself and gave birth to the answer. For the first time in my life, I felt that I had a solid grasp of enigmatic *parashas* Ha'azinu.

It traces the fearful change from *giluy panim* to *hester panim*, from God's open and unabashed directing Jewish life to His withdrawal into Himself where, hidden from undeserving eyes, he would continue to look after us but differently and from afar.[6]

It seems to me that the very same system, the throwback to an idyllic past with the purpose of underscoring the contrast to a present marked by pain and sorrow, can be recognized in Yirmiyahu. His opening prophecy, the one which is immediately followed by the almost unrelieved lament which colors his vision,[7] speaks of the euphoria of the early love between God and His people: *I well remember the devotion of your youth, the love which enveloped us as we first came together, how you followed Me into the desolate wilderness. Israel was holy to HaShem, the firstfruits of His harvest.*

Both the opening passages of *parashas* Ha'azinu and the Yirmiyahu passages seem to have the same purpose. They are meant to provide a benchmark against which subsequent developments were to be measured. They convey the message that the *hester panim* which casts such a shadow over our lives is an aberration. It is not what the Ribono shel Olam had wanted for His world. It leaves mankind marking time when not actually regressing, instead of moving forwards towards *Acharis HaYamim*, the End of Days, when history as we know it will have run its course.

When we discuss God's providence, His *hashgachah* over our lives, the two modes of *giluy panim* and *hester panim* are major players. Clearly, *giluy panim*, literally "the face revealed," posits an open, no-holds-barred involvement while *hester panim*, literally "the face hidden," must obviously be satisfied with something very much less. We will use the next chapter to nail down these propositions. With that in place, we will be ready to examine some of Ramban's ideas concerning *hashgachah*.

*L*et me share with you what were probably the worst ten minutes of my life. It was during the Gulf War, and I was sitting in the car with the radio on. They interrupted the program with the news that a Scud had just lifted off and was due to make contact in Eretz Yisrael in about ten minutes. I don't recall what I did. Perhaps I said Tehilim, perhaps I did not. What I do remember is the feeling of helplessness, the awful fear of what might happen in the next few moments. I do not have the eloquence to make the experience real for you. Everyone can fill in the details for himself.

I am writing this essay on the train. I am typing on my laptop with my cell phone lying ready beside me. The world is at my fingertips. Let me tell you some of the thoughts that have been meandering through my rather unfocused mind during the last half hour. I have long maintained that Thomas Edison should rank high on any list of the villains of the last century. With the invention of the incandescent bulb, he banished the natural rhythms of nights and days from our lives. Our grandfathers went to bed with the setting sun and were up to greet its friendly face in the morning. People lived natural lives, worked hard and rested well. They functioned as denizens of Earth, lived as the Ribono shel Olam had planned for them. The electric bulb changed all that. Who knows to what extent the pathology of our sick society is rooted in the havoc which the bulb has played with our structured lives?

Today's widely available instant communications have had as negative an impact on society as the electric bulb did in its day. Edison deprived us of our time; the computer denies us our space. We used to live in villages, met a couple of thousand people throughout our lives, were able to join them honestly in their joys and truly mourn with them in their sorrows. We had room in our hearts to make all our acquaintances at home there. Now things are different. There is simply no space to accommodate the entire world. Our feelings are deadened by intolerable overload. We cannot possibly dance at every *chasunah* or weep at every funeral. We have lost what may well be the most basic element of our humanity. Our ability to care has been diminished and we, we have been diminished together with it.

Why did the Ribono shel Olam permit this to happen? Does He want us to live such unnatural lives?

Perhaps He does. Let us remember that we are living in *golus*. There is certainly nothing that is less natural for Klal Yisrael than the exile existence. Let us listen to the Torah's description of *golus*.

והיו חייך תלאים לך מנגד ופחדת לילה ויומם ולא תאמין בחייך:
בבקר תאמר מי יתן ערב ובערב תאמר מי יתן בקר מפחד לבבך אשר תפחד
וממראה עיניך אשר תראה:

Your very life will taunt you with its uncertainty, you can never be certain of your nights or your days. Come morning and you will wish that last night had never passed. Come evening and you will remember the morning with nostalgia. You will be in the grips of fear; the things you see will not leave you in peace.

Is this true for our *Golus America*? Certainly not. We are unafraid and enjoy a life which by any standard would have to be described as one of security and luxury. Even the occasional, sharp reminder that we are still very much in *golus* does not alter the basic truth. Things are very good for us.

So why do I rush to the computer to check out the news from Eretz Yisrael the minute Shabbos is out? Why is our mailbox stuffed every day with so much pain? Why do we all never tire of discussing whether things have really changed for the worse? Is it simply a matter of better communications which make us aware of situations which in other circumstances we would never have encountered. Why so many outstretched hands? Why so many whys?

Perhaps the Ribono shel Olam is bringing all these *tzoros* to our doorstep in order to teach us that we are never to ask, "Which Jew is in trouble this time?" If an aching heart around the corner or a thousand miles away does not pain me, if distance mutes for me the sound of a choking sob because I cannot hear it, then it is I who am in trouble. It is I who am not fully, Jewishly, alive.[1] God wants us to know that *golus* does not require dark and narrow ghettoes, a preening peasant and an oppressive *poritz*, yellow stars and filthy spittle in our faces. *Golus* is *pizur*, being scattered, each of us feeling safe in an individual cocoon. It is the attenuation of the collectivity which we call *Klal Yisrael*, a concept which makes all of us into a single organism in which each part is closely bound to every other.

So we are all still very much in *golus*. Let us see whether, in historical terms, we are able to give some conceptual body to our current, relatively benign, exile experience.

We will need to study the following passage in VaYeileich (Devarim 31:16–18):

טו. ויאמר יהוה אל משה הנך שכב עם אבתיך וקם העם הזה וזנה אחרי אלהי נכר הארץ אשר הוא בא שמה בקרבו ועזבני והפר את בריתי אשר כרתי אתו.

יז. וחרה אפי בו ביום ההוא ועזבתים והסתרתי פני מהם והיה לאכל ומצאהו רעות רבות וצרות ואמר ביום ההוא הלא על כי אין אלהי בקרבי מצאוני הרעות האלה.

יח. ואנכי הסתר אסתיר פני ביום ההוא על כל הרעה אשר עשה כי פנה אל אלהים אחרים.

16. HaShem said to Moshe, "When you go and lie with your ancestors, this nation will rise up and stray after the alien gods of the land to which they came. They will thus abandon Me and violate the covenant which I made with them.

17. "On that day I will allow My fury to be kindled against them and abandon them. *I will hide My face from them*, and they will fall prey to their enemies. Beset by many evils and troubles, they will say, 'It is because my God is no longer with me that these evils have befallen us.'

18. "On that day I will utterly *hide My face* because of all the evil that they have done in turning to alien gods."

The story is one of abandonment. Here is the background.

Israel will be inexorably drawn to the idol worship of Canaan in complete disregard to the covenant that they had forged with the Ribono shel Olam (verse 16).

God will become angry and hide His face from them (*hester panim*) and, as a result, they will be exposed to all manner of terrible suffering. This will bring them to their senses and they will come to the realization that their pain came about as a direct result of the fact that they had, so to speak, driven God out of their midst (verse 17). When the Jews come to this realization, God will once more hide His face from them. This, because of the sin they had committed in serving the alien gods (verse 18).

The problems raised by these verses are self-evident. Verse 17 clearly posits some degree of *teshuvah*, repentance. Even if we grant that an admission of guilt does not go far enough, it is still clear that, at the very least, a beginning has been made. Why, then, should verse 18 predict a further *hester panim*? Moreover, the double *haster astir* implies that this second "hiding of the face" is to be more severe than the earlier one. Are we then to assume that the partial *teshuvah*, far from making things better, is really a regression?

There is a third difficulty. Verse 18 makes clear that the second *hester panim* is to come as a result of their earlier idol worship. Clearly, then, no significant fault is to be found after the initial *teshuvah*. There appears to be a residue from the earlier disloyalty which demands this renewed distancing of the Divine Presence. Are we able to identify what this might be?

We will have to study Ramban at Devarim 31:18.

וטעם ואנכי הסתר אסתיר פני פעם אחרת, כי בעבור שההרהרו ישראל בלבם
כי חטאו לאלהים ועל כי אין אלהיהם בקרבם מצאום הרעות האלה, היה ראוי
לרוב חסדי השם שיעזרם ויצילם שכבר כפרו בע"ז, וכענין שאמר (ירמיה ב לה)
הנני נשפט אותך על אמרך לא חטאתי:

ולכך אמר, כי על כל הרעה הגדולה שעשו לבטוח בע"ז יסתיר עוד פנים
מהם, לא כמסתר פנים הראשון שהסתיר פני רחמיו ומצאום רעות רבות וצרות,
רק שיהיו בהסתר פני הגאולה, ויעמדו בהבטחת פני רחמיו (ויקרא כו מד) ואף
גם זאת בהיותם בארץ אויביהם לא מאסתים ולא געלתים וגו' עד שיוסיפו על
החרטה הנזכרת וידוי גמור ותשובה שלימה, כמו שנזכר למעלה (ל ב) ושבת
עד ה' אלהיך וגו' :

The sense is that that the Ribono shel Olam will hide His face a second time. Now, since the Jews had already realized that they had sinned against God and admitted to themselves that these evils came upon them because their God was not among them, we might have expected that God in His great mercy would aid them and save them. They had, after all, already denied the idols which they had worshipped. Yirmiyahu (2:35) taught that God's anger is kindled against people who deny having sinned. They were no longer in denial.

It is in order to answer this question that the Ribono shel Olam explains that because the evil in their trusting the idols was so great, He will once more hide His face from them. However, this time, the withdrawal will be of a different order. Earlier, God had hidden His attribute of *mercy*, with the result that the people were overtaken by all kinds of suffering. This time it is not the attribute of mercy which will be hidden but all knowledge concerning the ultimate redemption. . . . This will not be revealed to them until they accomplish a perfect *teshuvah* as described above (Devarim 30:2).

Ramban tackles the first of our problems head-on. The earlier *hester panim*, the withdrawal of God's attribute of mercy, had served its purpose and was no longer necessary. The Ribono shel Olam was ready to treat us with a full measure of His kindness and goodness. The dreadful suffering that had earlier smothered and smashed us had become a thing of the past. The second *hester panim* was of a different order entirely. It decreed that we would remain in the dark concerning the ultimate redemption. Our remaining exile years would have to be energized by belief and hope and prayer but not by knowledge. Our hearing would not be sufficiently acute to perceive the footsteps of Moshiach.

While Ramban does not address our other two problems directly, I believe that we can build upon what he does say. We wondered why God's intensification, evidenced by the doubling *haster astir*, was required for the second *hester panim*. Once we realize that the Ribono shel Olam's attribute of mercy was now at full strength, it becomes clear. The Ribono shel Olam, as it were, had to suppress His inclination towards mercy if He were to keep the secrets of redemption hidden. A father, aching to gather his once wayward son into his embrace, must struggle with himself if he realizes that such no-holds-barred acceptance is not yet appropriate. God had to be utterly determined to prolong specific aspects of the *hester panim* if He were not to give in to the promptings of His *midas harachamim*, His attribute of mercy.

Now, why *was* it so important that the *face of redemption* remain hidden? I believe that the Ramban provides the answer through a very careful choice of words. In explaining the second *hester panim*, he speaks of the evil in their *trusting* the idols, not in *serving* them. It is a sinful *act* to serve idols. It is a poisonous *attitude* to place one's trust in them. Once a firm enough decision has been taken, it becomes relatively easy to cease and desist from performing a deed. It is a much longer and much more difficult process to shake a misguided attitude. We need to be subjected to a long and painful therapy in which idol after idol is smashed, in which all our imagined support systems are shown to be mirages before we are ready to come out to meet our Moshiach.

It takes a *navi,* a prophet, to attach an authoritative definition to an entire historical period. I certainly can lay no claim to have my ideas even considered seriously. Still, I will share with you some thoughts which passed through my mind as I was writing this essay.

We also know, however, that our present exile around the world, whether in America, Israel or Europe, is much, much easier to bear than were any other exiles throughout history. Is it perhaps possible that from the horrors of the Holocaust a sufficient *teshuvah* was generated that we collectively said, "It is because my God is no longer with me that these evils have befallen us?" Is it possible that as a community we have left the earlier *hester panim* behind and are already living through the next stage? Could it be that all we have to do is to wean ourselves away from the trust which we place in so many and varied "idols" and that then we will be ready to welcome Moshiach into our midst?

These are questions which I will not attempt to answer. I will leave them to you, dear Reader, to contemplate as we move forward to analyze the concept of *hester panim* a little further.

he *locus classicus* for the study of *hester panim* is Chagigah 5b. The *sugia* takes up no more than a few lines,
but studied carefully and lovingly, it yields profound
insights into our history and our present standing with
the Ribono shel Olam. Whatever our subsequent study of *hashgachah* will yield, it will be colored by what we will have uncov-
ered in this chapter.

Here is the Gemara:

ואנכי הסתר אסתיר פני ביום ההוא, אמר רבא: אמר הקדוש ברוך הוא: אף
על פי שהסתרתי פני מהם–**בחלום אדבר** בו. רב יוסף אמר: ידו נטויה עלינו,
שנאמר ובצל ידי כסיתיך.

On that day I will utterly hide My face (Devarim 31:18). Rava
taught: God declared, "In spite of the fact that I have hidden My face from them, I will yet speak to them [lit. him] in
a dream. Rav Yosef demurred.[1] He taught: His hand will be
stretched out over us, as it is written, *I have covered you with
the shade provided by My hand* (Yeshayahu 51:16).

As described in note 1, the text as we have it implies that R. Yosef
disagrees with Rava. We also noted that Turei Even emends the
text such that there is no implication of any argument. Rashi does
not indicate which reading he had. Dikdukei Sofrim has no vari-
ant recensions so we must assume that Turei Even is the first one
to suggest a different reading. It therefore seems that Rashi accepts
that Rav Yosef disagrees with Rava. Let us examine what their argument might be.

On the words, *I will yet speak to them in a dream*, Rashi comments: "I will appear to him (any one of them) in a dream to show
him the troubles which lie in store so that they will be inspired
to pray." On R. Yosef's idea of the outstretched hand, Rashi comments, "[The hand is outstretched] so that it might protect us."

If now we assume, as indeed we must, according to the generally accepted text, that R. Yosef argues with Rava, we would probably have to assume the following disagreement. R. Yosef believes that Rava's concept of *hester panim* is too liberal. If the Ribono shel Olam is still communicating with us, albeit in the hazy dream world, it would hardly be correct to say that His "face" is "hidden." Rather, R. Yosef maintains that during *hester panim* there will be no communication at all. Nevertheless we will not be abandoned. God's "hand" will still be stretched over us, making sure that we are protected.

In order to understand things a little better, let us first see whether we can find a more thorough understanding of the *hand* which, as R. Yosef sees it, still protects us.

Maharsha can help. He marshals sources which indicate that when the word *yad* is used, it always refers to the left hand. Furthermore, he notes that the right hand is associated with God's faculty of mercy; conversely God imposes unmitigated justice with the left hand. Now Eichah 2:3 tells us that *He has withdrawn His* RIGHT *hand in the presence of the enemy*. Rashi explains that this means that God no longer uses His right hand to fight those who attack us. I imagine that Maharsha would read this to mean that in our exile God will still battle for us but only with the left hand of justice. In contrast to the past when God protected us with much more force than we really deserved (mercy), He now does only the bare minimum which justice requires.

Now what does justice require of the Ribono shel Olam? He has a contract with us that *even when they are in the lands of their enemies, I will not grow so disgusted with them, nor so tired of them, that I would destroy them and break My covenant with them....* (VaYikra 26:44). R. Yosef maintains that *hester panim* implies something much darker than Rava described. There will be no communication at all but still God will abide by His obligations. The "left" hand will fight our enemies but only as hard as may be required to ensure that we not be destroyed. Beyond that—nothing.

I have the feeling that while Rava and R. Yosef may disagree, it is still possible that their respective stands are not mutually exclusive.

Here is my suggestion.

There is a remarkable discussion of *giluy panim* versus *hester panim* in the Meshech Chochmah to Shemos 3:13–14. It is too long and complex to make it possible to offer even a shortened version here, but, in my opinion, it is a *must* for anybody who is interested in the topic and can handle it. Here is one truncated sentence, abstracted from the whole beautiful and imposing structure:

כשההשגחה היא בהסתרת פנים . . . אז הוא בבחינת שמוני בניך כחולדה
הדרה בעקרי בתים (פסחים קיח):

When God's providence is exercised in a state of *hester panim*, then it may be described with the words used in Pesachim 118a in a complaint made by *Kenesses Yisrael*[2] to the Ribono shel Olam, "Your children have made me exist as does a weasel lodged in the foundations of the house."

If I understand the Meshech Chochmah correctly, he interprets the metaphor as describing an invisible presence, something that is known to exist but is never seen. In that sense, it might be an exact description of the Ribono shel Olam during periods of *hester panim*. We know Him to be there, but He will not permit us to apprehend His stewardship of the world's affairs.

I suspect that many of us, particularly those among us who have at one time or another employed an exterminator, would read the metaphor just a little differently. Rodents hidden somewhere in the house tend to make their presence felt by the occasional foray into the open. If we could never see them, we would not mind so much. It is the occasional predatory excursion which makes them so uncomfortable for us.

Perhaps then, Kenesses Yisrael might be complaining to the Ribono shel Olam that the actions of His children have condemned it to a weasel-like existence. Only occasionally does Kenesses Yisrael act as would be expected from the exalted fellowship to which it belongs, thus emerging from its hiding place and allowing it to be seen, unashamedly, by all. Most of the time, judging by Jewish actions, no one would suspect that such an entity even exists. It is tucked away, and only the cognoscenti even know of its presence.

If all this is correct, it should be possible to accommodate the views of both Rava and R. Yosef. Rava's opening for some form of communication in spite of *hester panim* might be applicable to times when Kenesses Yisrael is out in the open. Rav Yosef's more restrictive interpretation would hold true for such times as it has to remain concealed. The language of the Gemara which implies that there is a disagreement would still be true. The target of R. Yosef's demurral would be Rava's apparently undifferentiated assertion that *hester panim* would *never* block out communication altogether, that the dream world would *always* remain open. R. Yosef claims that room must also be found for the lesser involvement implied by the Yeshayahu verse. When Kenesses Yisrael will have been driven into its cellar-lair, there would be nothing at all to break the dreadful silence in spite of the fact that even then God would be protecting us under his outstretched arm.

If we would be willing to widen Rava's "I will yet speak to them in a dream," beyond Rashi's interpretation, this Gemara could prove to be an enormous help to us as we grapple to understand the chaotic times in which we live. We recall that, as Rashi explains, Rava's idea is that even during periods of *hester panim*, God will send us dreams which would stimulate us to repentance. I have heard it suggested that Rava might be interpreted more broadly. Perhaps he means that although God will not manifest Himself clearly, as it were, in full color during periods of *hester panim*, we will nevertheless be able to discern him in a hazy, dreamlike manner. We will be able to perceive that *something* momentous is happening, that beyond any doubt God is directing things from behind a distorting screen, that He is "there" although we cannot grasp Him fully any more than we are able to recognize clearly the actors who people our dreams.

Looking back at the events that happened during my own lifetime, the disagreement between Rava and R. Yosef helps categorize them effectively. As partners with the Ribono shel Olam in history we can (begin to) discern intelligible patterns within the many cosmic tremors which have punctuated the last century. Certainly there were the dreadful times in which the Divine silence posited by R. Yosef seemed impenetrable. With Esther feeling all alone as she entered the fearful palace, we cried out, *My God, my God, why have You abandoned me; why are You so far from delivering me and from my anguished cries?* (Tehilim 22:1; see Megillah 15b). We knew that somewhere God was watching and planning, knew beyond any doubt that somewhere in the inscrutable future, a light must be beckoning. At the same time, nevertheless, we felt that our experiences seemed to be confirming R. Yosef's ideas more than those of Rava.

There were, however, many occasions when, although we fell short of experiencing actual prophecy, the voice of God was nevertheless audible to us from within the crash and splendor of history.[3] As the late R. Soloveitchik pointed out, the president who was wielding the gavel at the United Nation's partition vote in 1948 was not some hapless politician but the Ribono shel Olam Himself. Who else could have brought Russia and the United States together on such a significant issue? Who, if not the Ribono shel Olam Himself, fought the battles which pitted 600,000 Jews, many of them Holocaust survivors, against the surrounding Arab populations numbering fifty million? Who preserved us during the miraculous six days in '67, and Who helped us to rally after the dreadful early blows which we sustained in the Yom Kippur War?

The list can go on and on. Happy are we that, in spite of the *hester panim* which is indigenous to our *golus*, we still have so many opportunities to catch a fleeting glimpse of the Ribono shel Olam watching out for us.

And yet, even those precious moments lack absolute clarity. They have a dreamlike quality which makes them hazy and indistinct. Nobody can say with anything near certainty that he has understood the message correctly. Even the establishment of the Jewish state has evoked reactions among good and holy people which range from unbounded joy and gratitude to the Ribono shel Olam for having wrought this miracle to an utterly negative attitude which views, and therefore mourns, its almost unrelieved secularism as a Jewish travesty.

15 : WHEN THISTLES
GROW IN GOD'S VINEYARD

e cannot begin to think about Ramban's ideas concerning *hashgachah*, God's providential knowledge, caring and active involvement in every aspect of our lives,[1] without first quoting his own ringing affirmation, which we find at Shemos 13:16.

Here is a paraphrase of what he says:

ומן הנסים הגדולים המפורסמים אדם מודה בנסים הנסתרים שהם יסוד התורה כלה, שאין לאדם חלק בתורת משה רבינו עד שנאמין בכל דברינו ומקרינו שכלם נסים אין בהם טבע ומנהגו של עולם, בין ברבים בין ביחיד, אלא אם יעשה המצות יצליחנו שכרו, ואם יעבור עליהם יכריתנו ענשו, הכל בגזרת עליון כאשר הזכרתי כבר.

The major upheavals which to any unprejudiced mind are clearly miraculous point to the necessary corollary that we are also constantly exposed to hidden miracles. This belief is fundamental to Judaism. No one can claim a part in the Torah of Moshe Rabbeinu unless he believes that *whatever happens* to both individual and community partakes of the miraculous. It is never a matter of nature simply taking its course. If a person observes the commandments his reward will bring him success; if he violates them his punishment will cause his extinction. It is all by the decree of the Most High. . . .

It all sounds simple enough. If our experiences occasionally make us wonder to what extent these theories actually play themselves out in the real world, that puts us in good company. The question of the suffering of the righteous and the tranquillity of the wicked is not of our invention. Iyov spent a lot of time wondering about just this conundrum, as did Dovid HaMelech in Tehilim, Shlomo HaMelech in Koheles, Chabakuk in his prophecies and many, many writers and thinkers throughout our history. Many answers have been hazarded; many of them can help a great deal. I suspect that none of them will satisfy our searching in every problematic circumstance but, taken together, they probably provide reasonable explanations in most cases.

In this essay, I propose to leave the hurly-burly of the "street," the home, the marketplace and the community and, instead, ask the Ribono shel Olam Himself. He has revealed in TaNaCh as much of Himself as He wishes us to know. It is there that we shall go to learn how He deals with His frequently wayward children. If the answers which He provided for us seem to throw some of the Ramban's assertions into question, then we will at least be able to tackle the issue in the quiet of the Beis HaMidrash instead of having our emotions roiled by the live and troubling human question marks which sneak around in our communities and, there in the marketplace, tend to wreak such havoc with our certainties.

We go to Yeshayahu, chapter 5, to see what we will be able to find.

א. אשירה נא לידידי שירת דודי לכרמו כרם היה לידידי בקרן בן שמן:
ב. ויעזקהו ויסקלהו ויטעהו שרק ויבן מגדל בתוכו וגם יקב חצב בו ויקו לעשות ענבים ויעש באשים:
ג. ועתה יושב ירושלם ואיש יהודה שפטו נא ביני ובין כרמי:
ד. מה לעשות עוד לכרמי ולא עשיתי בו מדוע קויתי לעשות ענבים ויעש באשים:
ה. ועתה אודיעה נא אתכם את אשר אני עשה לכרמי הסר משוכתו והיה לבער פרץ גדרו והיה למרמס:
ו. ואשיתהו בתה לא יזמר ולא יעדר ועלה שמיר ושית ועל העבים אצוה מהמטיר עליו מטר:
ז. כי כרם יהוה צבאות בית ישראל ואיש יהודה נטע שעשועיו ויקו למשפט והנה משפח לצדקה והנה צעקה:

1. I will stand in for my beloved to sing the song which he, my friend, sang to his vineyard. For my beloved owned a vineyard which grew in a lush and fertile place.

2. He had broken the ground and cleared it of stones. He had planted it with choice vines and built a watchtower to protect it. He had even sunk a winepress into the ground. He had dreamed of luscious grapes, but instead it produced noxious fruits.

3. Now then you Dwellers of Yerushalayim, Men of Yehudah adjudicate, I beg you, between Me and My vineyard.

4. What more might I have done for My vineyard which I failed to do? Why when I had every right to anticipate luscious grapes did it instead produce noxious fruits?

5. Now I will tell you what I will do to my vineyard: I will remove the fencing so that animals will graze in it. I will break an opening in the wall so that it will be trampled.

6. I will turn it into a wasteland, it will be neither pruned nor hoed, thistles and thornbushes will grow. Moreover I will forbid the clouds to rain upon it.

7. For the family of Yisrael, the men of Yehudah are the vineyard of HaShem Tzevakos, they are the garden in which He took delight. He hoped for justice and instead found leprous distemper, for righteousness and instead heard the cries of the oppressed.

You, my dear Reader, deserve better than the wooden rendering which I offer. I read once that poetry translated relates to the original as a painting of a tree relates to the tree. It may be a great likeness but there is nobody at home. A body without a soul, a lark without its song.

I suppose that it is anyway presumptuous to attempt a translation of Yeshayahu. It is patently impossible to capture even a fragment of the pathos, the longing, the love and the sorrow of God's song to His people. We have lost before we have even begun. Let us then agree that we are ill served by this translation and just carry on from there.

So why a song? If the Ribono shel Olam wishes us to know that we have let Him down and that we will have to face the consequences of our failures, why not tell this to us in prose? While the answer to this question is not the main concern of this essay, we can still spend a few moments thinking about the use of poetry in communication.

What are the conditions under which a more prosaic form of expression is inadequate? Maharal (Nesivos Olam, Nesiv HaAvodah

12) feels that the choice of form is determined by the profundity of the experience. The more moving or significant the occurrence, the more unusual in its makeup and ramifications, the more deeply our emotions are called into play, the greater is the need for a heightened, more evocative style.

Accordingly, we can readily understand the need to couch both God's lament and Yeshayahu's resolve to give it voice in poetic idiom. For both, the anguish runs deep indeed. For God there is the dreadful sense of having been rejected and repudiated by His beloved children. For Yeshayahu, there is the grim determination to do what he must do to shake the listeners from their equanimity.

Although not limited to poetry, the use of the simile is certainly one of its significant tools. I am not sure whether when a simile is used it is a formal requirement that the object which is being compared must accommodate every single attribute of that to which it is equated. Certainly, it seems to me that our passage implies that the Ribono shel Olam will treat our disloyalty precisely as the vintner treats his recalcitrant vineyard (see verses 5 and 6 above.).

If so, our passage seems to contain profound implications for the Ramban's ideas concerning the Ribono shel Olam's *hashgachah*. We recall that Ramban maintains that *everything* that happens is directly determined by God. However, this passage seems to take a different position. It is true that the vintner takes certain positive steps. He removes the fencing and breaches the wall. Once he has done that, he appears to be uninvolved. He does not drive the animals to graze and to trample the vines underfoot. He certainly does not plant the thistles and thornbushes that flourish in the abandoned vineyard. All this happens in the natural course of events, unplanned and unguided.

To the extent that the comparison is precise, this surely implies that not everything which happens to us is directly determined by the Ribono shel Olam. There appears to be an allowance for happenstance *once we have distanced ourselves from the Ribono shel Olam to the extent that He no longer cares to protect us.* If life seems to trample us, if our path seems strewn with thorns and thistles, it may be happening not because of God's direct intervention but simply because that is how nature works upon those whom the Ribono shel Olam has deserted.

What would Ramban say to all this? Let us move on to the next chapter and see where our explorations will lead us.

16: THE RIBONO SHEL OLAM
IS WITH US—ALWAYS

*W*e have set ourselves a difficult task for this and the coming chapters. We are dealing with the delicate subject of *hashgachah*, God's involvement in and direction of all that happens in our lives. It is essential that we get it right. I call the subject delicate, because it matters so much to us just when we are at our most vulnerable. The knowledge that even in times of pain or sorrow we are still cradled, snug and safe, in the Ribono shel Olam's embrace is perhaps the most precious idea which we can carry, or better yet which can carry us, through life.

In the last chapter we came to the realization that we will have to tinker a little in order to refine this concept since not all sources seem to point in the same direction. We will take our time and do as thorough a job as we are able. Because I have the feeling that, in the end, it will be the Chazon Ish in his Emunah U'Bitachon who will take us where we need to go, I will begin our analysis with his affirmation at the beginning of the second chapter.

אבל ענין הבטחון הוא האמון שאין מקרה בעולם, וכל הנעשה תחת השמש
הכל בהכרזה מאתו ית׳ .

Bitachon is the belief that there is no such thing as happenstance. Whatever happens here on earth happens only because God ordained that it should be so.

We shall be coming back to this Chazon Ish and will then treat it in greater detail. In the meanwhile we should let the opposition speak. We will muster several sources which at first blush seem to reject this absolute position. They seem to contend that things may and do happen without being specifically willed by God.

An important source is the Chovos HaLevavos at the beginning of Shaar HaBitachon. Here is a paraphrase: *People need to trust someone; it is going to be either the Ribono shel Olam or someone else.*

God does not force His providence upon us. If we prefer to place our fate in other hands, He will go along with us. He will withdraw His own HASHGACHAH, *and leave us to our own devices.*[1] The implied threat comes through very clearly. Whoever you will trust other than the Ribono shel Olam will not be able to do much for you. You will find yourself adrift in a sea of happenstance. You will find out quickly enough how it feels to flounder outside the field of the Ribono shel Olam's involvement.

What would Ramban say to all this?

Here is another authority who, apparently in contrast to Ramban, finds no difficulty in envisaging life lived without the Ribono shel Olam's direct involvement. The Malbim posits that Shir HaShirim 1:7 offers the shepherd's interaction with his flock as a metaphor for God's direction of our lives. Two modes are postulated. The one, *tir'eh*,[2] describes what happens in the cool morning hours. The shepherd is actively and fully occupied with each sheep. He controls every aspect of their lives. Nothing that happens to any of them lies beyond the ambit of his concerns. However, this changes when the fierce afternoon sun begins to blaze. The heat produces lethargy and a new mode, *tarbitz*,[3] sets in. The shepherd has the sheep lie down at rest and stops worrying about the individual sheep. He will still keep an eye open for predators, making sure that the flock will not be killed off. But he shrugs off any other role.

In this metaphor, the morning stands for a time of an open, unimpeded relationship between God and His people while the oppressive heat of the afternoon describes a situation when God seems very distant and the physical world, typified by the sun,[4] is much in evidence. In the terms with which we became familiar in chapters 12 through 14, we would equate the morning with *giluy panim* and the afternoon with *hester panim*. In contrast to Ramban's assertion that *nothing ever* happens that is not the direct Divine decree of the Ribono shel Olam, Malbim seems comfortable with an "afternoon" marked by a much greater passivity than is consonant with Ramban's picture.

Up to this point in our presentation, we have provided what seemed to be a counterweight to Ramban's proposition. We all know that there can be profound disagreements about even the most basic issues and another *machlokes* would not create any significant problem for us. But, in the present situation, things are different. To our intense surprise, it is Ramban himself who seems most eloquently to contradict the passage which we quoted in the previous chapter. Here is a paraphrase of what he writes in *parashas* VaYeira, Bereishis 18:19:

ידיעת השם שהיא השגחתו בעולם השפל, היא לשמור הכללים וגם בני האדם
מונחים בו למקרים עד בא עת פקודתם אבל בחסידיו ישום אליו לבו לדעת
אותו בפרט, להיות שמירתו דבקה בו תמיד, לא תפרד הידיעה והזכירה ממנו
כלל כטעם לא יגרע מצדיק עיניו (איוב לו ז) ובאו מזה פסוקים רבים, כדכתיב
(תהלים לג יח) הנה עין ה' אל יראיו, וזולת זה.

God's knowledge of our physical world, that is, the providence which He dispenses, is limited to maintaining the universal rather than the individual. Even individual humans [as opposed to humanity as a whole] are subject to happenstance [literally *left to (the vagaries of) happenstance*] until the time when their fate will be visited upon them. However, [this is true of only ordinary people]. His *chasidim*, that is the most pious ones, are different. God considers them and is concerned for them even as individuals. He never for a moment relaxes his guardianship over them. . . .

Clearly our reading of the Ramban whom we quoted in the previous chapter must have been faulty. We cannot tolerate such a blatant contradiction in his writings. If we can work out a satisfactory solution, we may find that what Ramban says there can also accommodate the ideas of Chovos HaLevavos and the Malbim. It will all prove to be a matter of rethinking the assumptions which we have been making.

Here then is our question.[5] Does the Ribono shel Olam ever look away from us? Does he ever withdraw His providence from us? Are we occasionally the victims or beneficiaries of neutral, uncaring forces that are totally uninterested in us, that do what they do without reference to who or what might be affected? Or, ought we to assume, indeed are we perhaps obliged to assume, that everything that happens to us, whether it appears to us to be beneficial or harmful, comes about only because God explicitly willed that things should be just so?

Let us think about the following story. A little boy enjoys playing with matches. His father has told him many times that he could get badly hurt, but he refuses to listen. The father tries everything but after a while he runs out of options. He decides that he must allow the child to play with the matches and find out the hard way that it hurts when you get burned.

Clearly the father is not going to give the child a box of matches and then leave for the office. He certainly does not want the child to get badly hurt or to burn down the house. He will hide behind the drapes and see what happens. If he sees that the child's actions are going to give him a little burn on his finger, he will not interfere. It is this lesson which he wishes the child to learn. If, however, he sees that the child might get seriously hurt, he will come out from behind the curtain and take the matches away.

Let us assume that everything works out as it should and the child suffers a small burn on his finger. At this point we have to become philosophers. How are we to describe what happened? Who burned the child? Did the child do it to himself because it is he who struck the match, or are we to ascribe what happened to the father who chose not to exercise his option to intervene?

As a layman, I would say that both alternatives are legitimate; that it is simply a matter of looking at the same event from two possible but different viewpoints. However, it seems clear to me that if the Chazon Ish's standard that *Whatever happens here on earth, happens only because God ordained that it should be so* is to be applied, it would be correct to ascribe the responsibility to the father. It is certainly true that, to the extent that it is given to a human being to exercise control, he decided that the child was to be hurt.

Let us take a look at another small passage from the Chazon Ish. I present a paraphrase which, I believe, will bear out the thesis which we have just offered.

וכאשר האדם נפגש במקרה אשר לפי הנוהג שבעולם צפוי' אליו סכנה מדרכי הטבע לפחוד מטבעת העולם, וקשת רוחו ירפהו מלזכור שאין המקרה אדוניה

לנו ושאין מעצור לד' מלהושיעו **ולהכן מסבבים שיחליפו את כל המסובבים,**
וההבלגה בשעה הקשה הלזו ולהשרות בקרבו את האמת הידועה כי אין כאן
לפניו שום פגע רע מיד המקרה רק הכל מאתו ית' בין לטוב בין למוטב, ואשר
שרש אמונתו מפיגה פחדתו ונותנת לו אמץ להאמין באפשרות ההצלה, ושאין
לפניו נטיה לרעה יותר מנטיה לטובה, ענין זה יקראוהו מדת הבטחון.

Now when we feel ourselves to be in danger, our natural instinct is to be afraid. Threatened, we find it difficult to remember that we are not at the mercy of happenstance. We forget that all is in God's hands, that He is well able to help us if He wishes. We lose sight of the fact that there exists no independent set of givens which must inevitably bring about the consequence which we fear. *All givens can be changed such that, as a result of that change, the outcome will be entirely different from that which would have ensued had these changes not been made and [that the "inevitable" outcome] which we anticipate with so much trepidation was not really inevitable.*

Here we have the test of true belief. Honest *bitachon* will enable us to find strength in the knowledge that there is absolutely no reason to assume that the worst will necessarily come about. With God in charge, nothing at all is predetermined.

I have italicized the sentence which is most relevant to our thesis. The Chazon Ish postulates the existence of a set of givens which if they were to remain unchanged would result in some predictable outcome. His argument is not that whatever happens is directly delivered by the Ribono shel Olam Himself. Nature functions in accordance with its laws. Things come about because a confluence of conditions brings them into being. God's providence, His *hashgachah*, expresses itself in either willing that these conditions remain unchanged (that is, things are left to nature) or in freely changing them (that is, things are still left to nature but God changes nature). Whether He does the one or the other, the results are said to be brought about by His untrammeled will.

With this insight in hand, we can readily agree that there are really no contradictions between any of the sources which we have cited. Ramban in *parashas* Bo states unequivocally that none of us are ever the victims of happenstance. Chovos HaLevavos, Malbim and certainly Ramban himself in his remarks in *parashas* VaYeira, quoted above, agree. These three have only this in common: they believe that for certain people at certain times and under certain conditions, God's providence may be expressed by *not* interfering with the existing conditions.

We are now ready to move on to Ramban's more general treatment of *hashgachah*. We have much to do and far to go.

$\mathcal{T}$he conclusions which we reached in the last few chapters are going to be of great help to us as we analyze Ramban's ideas on *hashgachah*. Equipped with what we have learned, we will not make the mistake of assuming uncritically that his comments on a particular *pasuk* are meant to describe the norm which will actually govern our daily lives. We will always be awake to the possibility that what is being said describes an ideal, applicable only in times of *giluy panim*. Life on the ground may well be very different. However, in this essay we hope to show that at bottom, there is more commonality between the modes of *giluy panim* and *hester panim* than we might expect.

Ramban's ideas about sickness and its cures can serve as a springboard for our discussion. We will read him very carefully because we want very much to read him correctly. Here is an excerpt from his commentary to VaYikra 26:11.

והכלל כי בהיות ישראל שלמים והם רבים, לא יתנהג ענינם בטבע כלל, לא בגופם ולא בארצם, לא בכללם, ולא ביחיד מהם, כי יברך השם לחמם ומימם, ויסיר מחלה מקרבם, עד שלא יצטרכו לרופא ולהשתמר בדרך מדרכי הרפואות כלל, כמו שאמר (שמות טו כו) כי אני ה' רופאך וכן היו הצדיקים עושים בזמן הנבואה, גם כי יקרם עון שיחלו לא ידרשו ברופאים רק בנביאים, כענין חזקיהו בחלותו (מ"ב כ ב ב ג) ואמר הכתוב (דהי"ב טז יב) גם בחליו לא דרש את ה' כי ברופאים, ואילו היה דבר הרופאים נהוג בהם, מה טעם שיזכיר הרופאים, אין האשם רק בעבור שלא דרש השם אבל הוא כאשר יאמר אדם, לא אכל פלוני מצה בחג המצות כי אם חמץ:

אבל הדורש השם בנביא לא ידרוש ברופאים–ומה חלק לרופאים בבית עושי רצון השם, אחר שהבטיח וברך את לחמך ואת מימיך והסירותי מחלה מקרבך, והרופאים אין מעשיהם רק על המאכל והמשקה להזהיר ממנו ולצוות עליו:

וכך אמרו (ברכות סד) כל עשרין ותרתין שנין דמלך רבה רב יוסף אפילו אומנא לביתיה לא קרא, והמשל להם (במדב"ר ט ג) תרעא דלא פתיח למצותא פתיח לאסיא והוא מאמרם (ברכות ס) שאין דרכם של בני אדם ברפואות

אלא שנהגו, אילו לא היה דרכם ברפואות יחלה האדם כפי אשר יהיה עליו
עונש חטאו ויתרפא ברצון ה' , אבל הם נהגו ברפואות והשם הניחם למקרי
הטבעים.

The following may be taken as a general principle: When Israel, taken as a national entity,[1] acts as it should, the laws of
nature do not at all control what happens. Nothing is left to
happenstance, neither as it affects their persons nor as it affects their land. This holds true concerning both the experiences of the community and those of the individual. This is
so because God will bless their bread and their water such that
they will never become sick and will therefore never require a
doctor or any kind of medical intervention. When prophecy
was still part of daily life, righteous people who sinned and
consequently became ill would turn to the prophet. . . . What
possible role could doctors play in the home of one who lives
in accordance with God's will? . . .

Berachos 64a reports that for the entire twenty-two years
during which the great Rabba was Rosh Yeshiva, Rav Yosef never once felt the need to have a surgeon come to his
house . . . This accords with Berachos 60a . . . *People ought
not to depend on medical intervention at all*[2]; *it is just that they
got into the habit of going to doctors.* If they had not become
habituated to visit doctors, sickness would have struck only
as punishment for having sinned and the cure would have
come about whenever God willed it. However, once they began to seek medical attention, God let them have their way
and abandoned them to happenstance.

Ramban's statement is clear enough. Still, we will gain much by
tracing at least one of his references to its source. I refer to the
passage from Berachos 60a: *People ought not to depend on medical intervention at all, it is just that they got into the habit of going
to doctors.* The quote sounds as though it were an independently
standing aphorism. As a matter of fact, it is part of a larger prayer
and it will have much to tell us about the issues which are engag-
ing us in this series of essays. Here is the Gemara which quotes the
full text of the prayer:

אמר רב אחא הנכנס להקיז דם אומר יהי רצון מלפניך ה' אלהי שיהא עסק
זה לי לרפואה ותרפאני כי אל רופא נאמן אתה ורפואתך אמת לפי שאין דרכן
של בני אדם לרפאות אלא שנהגו אמר אביי לא לימא הכי דתני דבי רבי
ישמעאל ורפא ירפא מכאן שניתנה רשות לרופא לרפאות.

Rav Acha taught: When someone enters a doctor's office to have his blood let, he is to recite the following prayer: "May it be Your will, Lord my God, that this procedure be an efficient cure and that [through it] You will indeed cure me of my sickness. [I turn to You] because You are a faithful healer and the cures which You effect are truly cures. For people ought not to depend on medical intervention at all, it is just that they got into the habit of going to doctors."

Abbaye argues with Rav Acha: People ought not to say this prayer. Rabbi Yishmael has taught that the phrase, *he shall surely heal him*,[3] teaches us that doctors have permission to cure people.[4]

Strange, is it not? Our protagonist is sitting in the doctor's office about to reject the Ribono shel Olam as the direct source of the healing which he craves. He is doing precisely that which, so the Ramban assures him, will put the Ribono shel Olam out of the picture. Nevertheless, Rav Acha advises him to affirm that his cure will come from God and that the very process which he has only now set into motion is religiously aberrant. If he believes all this, why does he not just go home, take out his Gemara or Tehilim and commit himself to the attention of the true specialist who alone can cure him?

It appears to me that in order to understand this passage correctly, we must revert to what we learned in chapter 16 concerning *hester panim*. From the story of the child who enjoyed playing with matches, we learned that even in a situation in which the Ribono shel Olam is hidden from us-, we can nevertheless consider Him to be the proximate cause of whatever happens since He is fully able to direct matters from behind the curtain.

Let us accept this proposition and go on from there. We note the interesting formulation of the prayer, the words which we rendered: THAT THIS PROCEDURE (ESEK ZU) *should be an efficient cure.* Certainly there is the implication that it is the *esek,* the procedure itself, which is to cure the illness. Nevertheless, the text continues *and that* YOU *will indeed cure me.* So it appears to be God Himself, not the procedure, Who will do the job. We are forced to conclude that the prayer asks God to effect the cure by acting through the procedure. The Ribono shel Olam's involvement is moved back one step.

In a time of *giluy panim,* the procedure is unnecessary and would therefore never be attempted. The cure would come about because there would be a perfect congruence between God's will and the facts on the ground. However, during *hester panim* nature functions, or at least seems to function, independently.[5] Left to itself, it is capable of producing results which might be other than those which the Ribono shel Olam would really want. When that happens, God will intervene. He must, so to speak, bend nature to His will.

By equating the two time periods, the one in which people never visited the doctor and the other when it became the ingrained habit to do so, with the categories of *giluy panim* and *hester panim,* we are now able to suggest an alternative translation for the difficult words *ein darkon shel benei adam* in Rav Acha's prayer quoted above. Please take a moment to read note 2 for the explication of our problem. Throughout *shas* the phrase invariably means *people* DO *not.* Why then would Rav Acha use it when what he wishes to say is that *people* OUGHT *not?*

During a period of *giluy panim* people in fact did not go to a doctor. Why would they when they needed only to look around them to see the sick and the crippled healed by the simple, or not so simple, expedient of doing *teshuvah?* Hence, in an ideal world people *do not* go to the doctor. Rav Acha, however, lived long after *giluy panim* had become nothing more than a memory, if that. In his time, the natural reaction to illness was to seek medical intervention. Nevertheless, Rav Acha suggested an appropriate prayer for someone who was ill. He should ask God to break through the wall which hides His presence from our daily lives and change the natural efficacy of the doctor's treatment into a willed cure emanating from the Ribono shel Olam Himself.

*I*n chapter 15 we quoted Ramban that nothing at all happens in our lives that is not governed by the Ribono shel Olam's caring, all-encompassing *hashgachah*. That is a very far-reaching statement that should command our attention. In the present essay, we will focus upon the implications of the phrase which we have italicized in the following quote of that Ramban.

שאין לאדם חלק בתורת משה רבינו עד שנאמין בכל דברינו ומקרינו שכלם
נסים אין בהם טבע ומנהגו של עולם, **בין ברבים בין ביחיד.**

No one can claim that his ideas stem from the Torah of Moshe Rabbeinu unless he believes that whatever happens *to both individual and community* partakes of the miraculous.

I am interested in Ramban's mention of "individual" (hereafter, *yachid*) and "community" (hereafter, *tzibur*) as two discrete entities. Clearly, he views the *tzibur* as more than simply a conglomeration of individuals. The community, so he implies, has its own character and it, *qua* "*tzibur*," is the object of God's caring concern as much as is the *yachid*.

What, precisely, is the nature of this *tzibur*? Ramban to VaYikra 1:2 introduces us to the differences between property that is owned by a partnership and that which belongs to a community. In the former, each of the partners, even if there are thousands, is a part owner. In the latter, individuals lose their identity in what we could best describe as the *corporate entity* which is the *tzibur*. The *tzibur* owns its property as a corporation. The individual *as* individual has no share at all.

In this essay we will explore the differences between *yachid* and *tzibur* as the Ribono shel Olam exercises His *hashgachah* over them. We will supply a paraphrase of the passage which we will use as our text. It is the first section of the second *parashah* of *krias shema*.

יג. והיה אם שמע תשמעו אל מצותי אשר אנכי מצוה אתכם היום לאהבה
את יהוה אלהיכם ולעבדו בכל לבבכם ובכל נפשכם:

יד. ונתתי מטר ארצכם בעתו יורה ומלקוש ואספת דגנך ותירשך ויצהרך:

טו. ונתתי עשב בשדך לבהמתך ואכלת ושבעת:

טז. השמרו לכם פן יפתה לבבכם וסרתם ועבדתם אלהים אחרים והשתחויתם
להם:

יז. וחרה אף יהוה בכם ועצר את השמים ולא יהיה מטר והאדמה לא תתן את
יבולה ואבדתם מהרה מעל הארץ הטבה אשר יהוה נתן לכם.

13. If you obey all the commands which I am giving you this
day, to love HaShem your God and to serve Him *with all your
heart and with all your energies.*

14. Then I will grant you rainfall in the appropriate season,
the earlier and the latter rains, so that you may gather in your
grain harvest, your wine and your oil.

15. I will also provide grass in your fields so that your animals
will be able to graze. You will eat and you will be satiated.

16. Be extremely careful that your hearts not be deflected from
My service, causing you to stray and serve idols and prostrate
yourself before them.

17. Then the anger of HaShem will burn against you so that
He will close off the heavens so that there will be no rain,
the earth will withhold its bounty and you will very quickly
be lost from the land which HaShem gave to you (Devarim,
chapter 11).

We have italicized the phrase "with all your heart and with all
your energies," because Sifrei, quoted by Rashi, questions the
need for this phrase. Earlier, in the first *parashah* of *krias shema*
(Devarim 4:19) the Torah had already taught us that the heart and
all our energies need to be invested in God's service.[1] Why repeat it
here? Sifrei answers that the earlier *parashah*, written in the singular
(*levave*CHAH), addresses the *yachid*, while the latter one, written
in the plural (*levave*CHEM), addresses the *tzibur*. There is clearly
a difference between the two since rewards and punishments are
spelled out only regarding the *tzibur*.

Ramban uses this Sifrei to develop some of his ideas on *hash-*

gachah. Let us study his words very carefully. I will provide a para-phrase.

יג. בכל לבבכם ובכל נפשכם והלא כבר הזכיר בכל לבבך ובכל נפשך, אלא
אזהרה ליחיד ואזהרה לצבור, לשון רש"י מספרי (עקב יג) ובאור הענין, כי
השם לא יעשה הנסים תמיד, לתת מטר הארץ בכל עת יורה ומלקוש ולהוסיף
בדגן ובתירוש וביצהר ולהרבות גם העשב בשדה לבהמה או שיעצור השמים
וייבשו, רק על מעשה רוב העם, אבל היחיד הוא בזכותו יחיה והוא בעונו ימות
והנה אמר כי בעשותם כל המצות מאהבה שלימה יעשה עמהם את כל הנסים
האלה לטובה, ואמר כי בעבדם ע"ז יעשה עמהם אות לרעה כי הנסים לא יעשו
לטובה או לרעה רק לצדיקים גמורים או לרשעים גמורים, אבל הבינונים כדרך
מנהגו של עולם יעשה בהם טובה או רעה כדרכם וכעלילותם:

The explanation is as follows: [Ramban is setting out to ex-plain the Sifrei. He begins from the premise that the earlier *parashah* deals with the *yachid* and the latter with the *tzibur*. He wants to understand why the reward for acting correctly and the punishment for straying is spelled out only in the context of the *tzibur*, not in that of the *yachid*.] The miracle of always being provided with rainfall, of always bringing in bountiful harvest, of plentiful grass in the fields, or the lack of all these as a punishment for dereliction, will only be wrought for the nation as a whole depending on how the majority acts. However, the individual will be rewarded or punished for his merits or deficiencies without resort to the miraculous. Na-ture will be harnessed to make sure that what must happen will happen.

[Now Ramban turns to the phrase which we have italicized. The language implies that the rewards which are to follow con-scientious fulfillment of our duties will come about only if we act full-heartedly and at the highest pitch of enthusiasm. Anything less than that will not be worthy of reward within the meaning of the *parashah*. Ramban wonders whether a less than optimum performance would still be deserving of some measure of reward.] Now we are told that fulfillment of the *mitzvos* when it is motivated by a full measure of love will trig-ger these miraculous rewards and that idol worship will be punished by a process which is equally miraculous. The insistence upon the two polar opposites comes about because the Ribono shel Olam will resort to miracles only in order to reward perfect *tzadikim* or to punish incorrigible *resha'im*. Those who occupy the center will also be treated in accordance with their actions but only by the creative use of natural forces. Miracles are disallowed for people at the center.

Let us summarize: The second *parashah* of *krias shema* is concerned with the subject of reward and punishment as these are applied to the community rather than to the individual. At the communal level, we may expect the miraculous to happen but only where the community, as represented by the majority of its members, inclines to one of the two extremes. At the center, the community is treated as is the individual who deserves reward or punishment. God will see to it that what needs to happen happens, but He will act only by such means as will guarantee that Divine intervention cannot be discerned. Nature, not the supernatural, will be harnessed to bring about God's will.

It seems to me that we ought to contrast what Ramban says here concerning a community which lives its life at the center with what he says concerning the individual who does not rise to the level of the *chasid*.

RAMBAN TO DEVARIM 11:13	RAMBAN TO BEREISHIS 18:19
Concerning the community which does not rise to the level of *tzadikim gemurim*.	Concerning the individual who does not rise to the level of the *chasid*.
The insistence upon the two polar opposites comes about because the Ribono shel Olam will resort to miracles only in order to reward perfect *tzadi-*	Even individual humans are subject to happenstance until the time when their fate will be visited upon them. However, [this is true of only ordinary

kim or to punish incorrigible *resha'im*. Those who occupy the center will also be treated in accordance with their actions but only by the creative use of natural forces. Miracles are disallowed for people at the center.	people]. His *chasidim*, that is, the most pious ones, are different. God considers them and is concerned for them even as individuals. He never for a moment relaxes His guardianship over them. . . .

A careful comparison between the two passages yields that while the *individual* who does not make the grade may be subjected to happenstance (the Bereishis passage),[2] the *community* will always be treated in strict accordance with its actions (Devarim).[3] Why? Wherein does the difference between the *yachid* and the *tzibur* reside?

Here is a thought. I cannot prove that the comparison which I am about to make is valid, but I believe that it may have some merit. We must visit the moment when Yaakov's sons were suddenly confronted by the realization that Yosef, the brother whom they had wronged so badly, was now holding them in his power. Yosef, aware of their discomfiture, is determined to set their minds at ease. He tells them (Bereishis 45:7) that it was all the work of *hashgachah*. The Ribono shel Olam arranged things so that Yosef would precede his family to Mitzrayim so that he would be able to sustain them during the dreadful famine. He shocks us at Bereishis 45:8 by claiming, apparently against everything we know about *bechirah*, free choice, that the Ribono shel Olam had manipulated them into selling him. *Now, it is not you who sold me to this place. It is God.* Does this not play havoc with the whole idea of reward and punishment which is so basic to Torah thought? Were then the brothers simple automatons who had no other choice than to do what they did?

Abarbanel says just that. He cites Mishlei 21:1, *The king's mind is like channeled water in the hands of God; He directs it wherever He wishes*. Malbim, in his commentary to this verse, expands on this idea:

פלגי מים לב מלך–הגם שלב האדם הפרטי נתון ברשותו והבחירה בידו, לא
כן לב המלך–אחר שבבחירתו תלוי אושר הכלל, ואם יבחר בדרך רע ישחית
רבים ועצומים, לכן לבו זה הכללי הוא ביד ה' .

Although private people are in control of their minds, giving each person freedom of choice, a king's mind is different.
Since his decisions affect the well-being of an entire nation,
he is denied autonomy over his decisions. Where these affect
many people, it is God Who decides what the king is to do.

The brothers' decision to sell Yosef was to affect the entire Jewish
people. Such determinations are made by God.

It seems to me that we can use Malbim's reasoning to explain
the Ramban's differentiation between the *tzibur* and the *yachid* in
the matter of *hashgachah*. A *yachid* who cannot muster sufficient
trust in the Ribono shel Olam and therefore depends on his own
skills, his doctor's perspicacity, the economy's promise and all the
other support systems which nature provides liberally, will, so to
speak, have his wishes fulfilled. God withdraws His direct involvement and leaves him to the various systems in which he placed his
trust. The *tzibur* is too precious for that. Neither king nor fate can
be trusted with its well-being. Its destiny will always be guided directly by the Ribono shel Olam.

I have a daughter. She thinks deeply about all things Jewish and when I occasionally say something which seems to call some of her deeply felt and cherished ideas into question, she does not let it go lightly. She probes doggedly, questions fiercely and forces me into reassessing and refining my thinking. Often, under her relentless scrutiny, I am forced to reexamine my assumptions and to align them more closely with her more conventional suppositions.

Recently, I mentioned the Ramban from Bereishis 18:19 which I have cited in earlier chapters. To make things a little easier for you, dear Reader, I will quote the passage here.

ידיעת השם שהיא השגחתו בעולם השפל, היא לשמור הכללים וגם בני האדם
מונחים בו למקרים עד בא עת פקודתם אבל בחסידיו ישום אליו לבו לדעת
אותו בפרט, להיות שמירתו דבקה בו תמיד, לא תפרד הידיעה והזכירה ממנו
כלל כטעם לא יגרע מצדיק עיניו (איוב לו ז) ובאו מזה פסוקים רבים, כדכתיב
(תהלים לג יח) הנה עין ה' אל יראיו, וזולת זה:

God's knowledge of our physical world, that is, the providence which He dispenses, is limited to maintaining the universal rather than the individual. Even individual humans are subject to happenstance until the time when their fate will be visited upon them. However, [this is true of only ordinary people]. His *chasidim*, that is, the most pious ones, are different. God considers them and is concerned for them even as individuals. He never for a moment relaxes his guardianship over them. . . .

Now Ramban's assertion that the Ribono shel Olam does not extend His *hashgachah* to people who do not measure up as His *chasidim* does sound strange to our ears. It is certainly not what people are taught in our Yeshivos and Batei Yaakov. My daughter was particularly shocked by the idea. She spoke passionately about the thousands of sufferers who find comfort in the knowledge that the Ribono shel Olam knows best, that surely He exposed them to the terrible burdens which they are forced to endure in order to give them the chance to battle mightily and come out stronger and better in the end. Their many prayers, the tears which they shed and the *teshuvah* which they often undertake, are all predicated upon the assumption that God is intimately involved in every aspect of their experience. Tell them otherwise and you will have denied them the very underpinnings of their faith, you will have told them that they are so many straws buffeted by the impersonal wind instead of being beloved children cradled in the embrace of a loving but stern father.

This simply cannot, indeed must not, be allowed to be true. The reasonably sophisticated theological gymnastics which I performed towards the end of chapter 16 and which carried us through chapters 17 and 18, which affirm that for some classes of people God's providence will be less direct than we would really like, may have their place in the Beis HaMidrash. They are not much use in the raw and roiling realities on the ground. There must be a better way. Thus did my daughter argue.

She is of course right. Can Ramban have meant to put the whole of our prayerful relationship with the Ribono shel Olam into question? That of course cannot be, particularly since Ramban, in a number of different contexts, cites belief in the efficacy of prayer as proof that God constantly interferes with the normal progression of nature and comes to our aid miraculously. Although Ramban mentions this in his Chumash commentary, particularly at Bereishis 46:15, we will cite him from Toras HaShem Temimah (Rav Chavel's Kisvei HaRamban, volume 1, page 153), where his wording is slightly more expansive than in the Chumash commentary.

‏...לפי שמעולם לא התפלל אדם להקב"ה שיתן לו טובה או שיצילנו מרעה,
‏ולא קלל את אויביו בשם, עד שהאמין בנסים כולם כאשר אמרתי . . .

No man ever prayed to God asking Him to fill a need or to save him from trouble nor did anyone ever call down curses upon his enemy without believing that God is prepared to intervene in nature miraculously. . . .

Ramban's meaning is clear. Every time we pray, we are asking God to make something happen which would otherwise, had we not petitioned God at all, not have happened. This means that nature, left to herself, would have acted one way but because of our prayer, the Ribono shel Olam bends it to His will. Prayer has no meaning if we do not posit *hashgachah*. Is it possible that the simple Jew who has not risen to the level of *chasid* has no business importuning God?

We have asked some good questions. It seems to me that the questions are so good that the answers are already determined. We simply cannot take the Ramban's words about the simple folk at face value. I have tried long and hard to figure out what he really means. I believe that I have taken some useful and important steps towards solving the conundrum. It involves subjecting the text to a very careful analysis. Do not let me scare you off, dear Reader. Follow me in my search for clarity; it will be a rewarding trip.

Our first concern will be to understand what the phrase *until* THE TIME WHEN THEIR FATE WILL BE VISITED UPON THEM really means. It is borrowed from Yirmiyahu 46:21 and 50:27. The Hebrew for the capped section is *eis pekudosom*.[1] Now Metzudos on those two verses, based on Bemidbar 16:29, believes that the phrase denotes *the day of death*. If we were to assume that Ramban ascribes the same meaning, we would have to render the sentence *Even individual humans are subject to happenstance until they die.* There seems nothing intrinsically wrong with this translation. In fact, that is indeed how I translated it in earlier chapters until I began rethinking the matter as I was writing the present essay. Upon reflection it has become clear that while in the Yirmiyahu *pesukim* it serves well enough, here, in Ramban's disquisition, it does not really satisfy. What does *until they die* add to *even individual humans, are subject to happenstance*? Why would anyone have thought that the abandonment of the ordinary people to happenstance would somehow be lifted before their death?

Now, Targum to the Yirmiyahu passages renders עת פקודתם as *saaron pish'eihon*,[2] which means *until their evil will be visited upon them*.[3] If Ramban has this rendering in mind, then he would be saying the following: those who do not rise to the level of *chasidim* will be left to the exigencies of happenstance except during certain times. The times that the Ribono shel Olam will intervene are those He has set aside for either rewarding these people when they have earned such reward or punishing them when their derelictions demand it.

It turns out that the two ways of rendering *eis pekudosom* yield radically different results. If we would go with Metzudos, Ramban would be saying that those people who do not rise to the level of *chasidim never* fall under the Ribono shel Olam's direct *hashgachah*. If Ramban accepts Targum's interpretation, it would simply mean that these people are *occasionally* left to the vagaries of nature. There will be times when what happens to them will be directly brought about through *hashgachah* either to reward or to punish. During the intervening times they are left to their own devices.

It seems to me that a close reading of Ramban's description of what happens to CHASIDIM makes it clear that he used *eis pekudosom* in the sense that Targum understood it: *However, His chasidim, that is, the most pious ones, are different. God considers them and is concerned for them even as individuals.* HE NEVER FOR A MOMENT RELAXES HIS GUARDIANSHIP OVER THEM. . . . Why would the Ramban make an issue of the fact that the *hashgachah* over the *chasidim* is *constant* if not for the sporadic nature of the *hashgachah* for those who do not make the grade. If the ordinary folk were totally excluded from *hashgachah*, it would be sufficient to say that the *chasidim* do live under its aegis.

If we were to stop right here, much of what disturbed my daughter would already have been solved. There is nothing in what the Ramban writes which would put into question the wonderful examples of direct *hashgachah* which even ordinary people occasionally experience. There will be times in even the simplest person's life in which the Ribono shel Olam cradles him as an individual in the warmth of His embrace. Our intuitions need fear nothing from the Ramban which without our careful analysis sounded so threatening.

However, there is more. The questions which we raised above about the efficacy of prayer for those who, in Ramban's view, are *subject to happenstance* can now be answered with absolute assurance.

Before we do so, we have time for a short excursus which will give us the chance to probe the rationale behind Ramban's assertion that there is a difference between *chasidim* and lesser mortals in relation to the Ribono shel Olam's *hashgachah*. I believe that it has to be expressed in the following terms. The *chasid* is a person who lives a life of *deveikus, of cleaving* to the Ribono shel Olam.[4] He lives his life in God's presence and where God is close, nature holds no sway. That is what David sang in Tehilim 16:8,[5] *I have set HaShem before me always,* BECAUSE HE IS AT MY RIGHT HAND, I SHALL NOT FALTER.[6] For ordinary people, for those of us who cannot claim to be living their lives in constant awareness of God's presence, nature is a force with which we have to reckon.

But not, and here we come to the crux of the matter, when we are standing before God in prayer. The very act of prayer is defined by the Gemara as "speaking *in the presence of the King*" (Eiruvin 64a). Every Jew, even those among us who can make no pretense to living their lives in a constant state of *deveikus,* have a personal audience with the King every time they stand in serious prayer before Him. Everybody can become a *chasid* in shul!

As we come to the close of this chapter and, indeed, of this little book, we would do well to think about the words of the Reishis Chochmah which we are about to quote. In learning the Ramban, we have been introduced to a potentially disturbing system which deals with people who are "in" and others who are "out." This, for most of us, sounds threatening. Nobody wants to feel that the Ribono shel Olam would ever allow him to be subject to the vagaries of nature. We do not want to be a part of the "out" group. We want to feel that the Ribono shel Olam is personally interested in and involved with every aspect of our lives.

Reishis Chochmah deals with "ins" and "outs" in a different context and has some encouraging words for us. We offer a paraphrase of the most significant parts.

הכלל שאין לך דבר שלא יתוקן בתשובה, ומה שפירשו בזוהר שאינו תלוי
בתשובה הוא שתשובתו קשה, ואף זה מכלל קושי התשובה שמראים לו
שאינו תלוי בתשובה ואין לך דבר שעומד לפני התשובה, ואף אם שמעת שובו
בנים שובבים חוץ מפלוני כענין אלישע אחר, אל תחוש, שהרי אלישע אחר

סוף סוף נתקבל אפילו שלא שב כל שכן אם היה שב שהיה מועיל לו יותר
ויותר אלא שסגרו דלתי התשובה בפניו והיה צריך להפציר עד יפתח הפתח,
וזהו מה שאמרו ז"ל כל מה שיאמר לך בעל הבית עשה חוץ מצא. בעל הבית
דהיינו הקדוש ברוך הוא כל מה שיאמר לך עשה מהמצות עשה, חוץ מצא
שאם יאמר לך צא מביתי ואל תכנס כענין אלישע אחר, אל תשמע לו אלא
תכנס בתשובה כי הוא חשקו של בעל הבית, אלא שמטעה אותך. (ראשית
חכמה, שער הקדושה פרק י"ז)

There is no evil in the world which cannot be cured with *tes-huvah*. Texts which seem to imply that some failings are simply too heinous for *teshuvah* to help mean simply that the sinner will find it extremely hard to do *teshuvah*. But those of us who manage to truly repent will find forgiveness for their sins. . . . This is expressed by the Sages when, in Pesachim 86b, they teach, *Always do whatever your host asks you to do unless he tells yous to leave. Then you should not listen to him.* The *host* in this homily is the Ribono shel Olam, and we are bidden to obey all His commands. However, when He tells us, "Leave My house and never again enter," do not listen to Him. Crash into the house through *teshuvah*. That is really what the Host wants. When He told you to leave, He meant you to understand that your transgression was not a simple matter. Nonetheless, He will welcome you if you manage to find your way back.

Here we have it. If what Ramban taught sounds to our guilty ears like a form of caste system, that is not what the Ribono shel Olam wants us to feel. He hopes that, knowing that we have not measured up to the degree of *deveikus* which would place us among the "ins," we will fight long and hard to regain entry into His embrace. The degree to which we remain on the outside depends entirely upon ourselves. The Ribono shel Olam is waiting.

*I*n the last few chapters we have dealt exhaustively with the Ramban's analysis of Bereishis 18:19 where he maintains that direct, constant *hashgachah* is reserved for God's *chasidim*. I do really believe that, in softening the impact of this almost frightening Ramban, we have, as they say in Yeshivos, learned good *p'shat*. I feel satisfied with what we have accomplished. However, there is one more bit of unfinished business and that is to see if we can identify the "*chasidim*" upon whom God lavishes His constant, focused *hashgachah* and the "ordinary folk" for whom such direct involvement is more sporadic.

Using Ramban's own categories, we can word our task as follows. From chapter 16 where we began our analysis, we recall that except when considering His *chasidim*, God deals[1] with the universal rather than the individual.[2] There are people who lift themselves above the ordinary and there are those who do not. Those who do not make the grade remain units within the species, a part of the crowd. These are left to the vagaries of nature, swept along by neutral forces not custom fashioned to their needs.[3] Now here is our question: What are the requirements for becoming a part of the elite? What, in this particular context, defines the one who breaks out of the crowd and rises to the level of the individual?

It seems to me that we would do well to refresh our memory about what we learned long ago in chapter 5. It was in that chapter that we demonstrated that, after considering various other possibilities, Ramban concluded that the truth lay with the Targum's interpretation of Bereishis 2:7. This is how we defined Ramban's final position.

After Adam was formed from the earth he was already imbued with a brutish life force. He was alive possessing all those faculties which he shared with the animals, but he was not yet human. When God imbued him with the *soul which gifted him with life*, he began to speak. He became human. However, all the "animal" faculties which he had possessed before being imbued with humanity remained as they were. They are essentially brutish. God ordained that they were always to be kept subordinate to the soul which God breathed into him.

God created man such that the "animal" within him remained "animal," as it had been, but that it was to be subordinated to the soul. In chapter 4 we showed that when that balance was disturbed, when the "animal," so to speak, slipped its leash, degeneration could follow very fast. I believe that these ideas can help us to answer our question.

Let us define "His *chasidim*" as people who maintain the balance between soul and body as the Ribono shel Olam had intended it, that is, that the "animal" part of man is always kept subordinate to his Godlike essence. The general category of ordinary people would then be those who have allowed their physical selves to get out of hand and who are identified more with their bodies than with their souls.[4]

Our task is now to find a theoretical framework within which the issue of whether or not a person might merit individual *hashgachah* is to be determined. Here is a hint. "Humans" count as individuals, "animals" do not. Let us proceed from that premise.

The best route by which we can familiarize ourselves in this arcane field is to take a glance at the Sefer HaIkarim 1:11. I will not even attempt a translation but will offer a short but by no means exhaustive paraphrase of the general thesis which he propounds.

ויובן מזה ג"כ שידיעת השם מקפת בדברים האישיים ובדברים הכלליים ולהורות ע"ז תמצא כי כשהקב"ה נגלה על בני נח שופך דם האדם באדם דמו ישפך כי בצלם אלהים עשה את האדם (בראשית ט') לרמוז על שהידיעה הפרטית דבקה באדם שאם לא היתה בו ידיעה כללית **כמו בשאר ב"ח לשמור המין בלבד** מה טעם שיהרג הרצח וכי ההורג אדם אחד הוא הורג כל המין אבל יאמר כי לפי שנעשה אדם בצלם אלהים הנה הוא קיים באיש וההורגו ראוי לעונש אחר שהידיעה האלהית הפרטית דבקה בו מצד הכח השכלי אשר בו כעליונים אשר הם קיימים באיש והידיעה הפרטית דבקה בהם מצד הכח השכלי שבהם וע"כ היה האדם ראוי לשכר ולעונש הפרטי המיועד בתורה.

Ikarim sets out to demonstrate that people, *as opposed to animals*, have individual worth. It would not occur to anybody that killing an animal would carry the death penalty but murdering a person does. The explanation must be that animals are valued only as part of a species. As long as the species remains, the death of the individual animal has no significance. Every human being, because of the uniqueness of his soul, is, so to speak, a species of one. When he is murdered, that species has disappeared forever.

The Ikarim makes it clear that the difference between humans and animals is expressed in the singularity of each human in contrast to the animal world which is comprised of the different species but not of the individual animal.[5]

From here to the Ramban which we are discussing is only a small step. Let us call the Ramban's *"chasid"* human[6] and the others "animal"[7] and everything falls into place. The Ribono shel Olam is interested in the *"chasid"* as an individual because he *is* an individual. All others fall into the "animal" category and as such can lay claims only as members of their species.

A word is in place here about the use of the word "animal" to describe human beings. If the word "animal" were being used in its usual sense, this would be an inexcusable offense against the Torah standard of *kavod haberios*. Every person, as person, is imbued with the Godly image with which the Ribono shel Olam endowed us. Any derogatory description is disallowed not only on the level of simple *menschlichkeit* but also as a matter of *halachah*.

Because of this, I have, wherever appropriate, placed the word "animal" in quotes in order to stress that I have a very specific meaning in mind. That meaning should be no more offensive than, for example, dividing creatures into animal, vegetable and mineral, and including humans in the animal category.

When I use this expression in the present context, I mean the following: As we determined in chapter 5, Ramban assumes that, in every person, there is a physical component which, before the Ribono shel Olam breathed the *nishmas chaim* into Adam, functioned in its own right at the level of all the animals which were created on the sixth day. After Adam was imbued with a *nishmas chaim,* this component remained part of him, but the Torah makes clear that it is to be subordinate to the human element. We refer to this physical component as "animal" only in this sense. When we allow this component of ourselves to slip its leash, we may be said to be giving free reign to the "animal" within us.

It is thus that the Ramban which we are about to quote should be understood.

Before we can suggest this as the solution for the difficult Ramban which we are discussing, we must determine whether he would agree that people who do not act as "humans" should act, might be described as "animals." We are particularly fortunate that there is indeed a passage in the Ramban where he does just that. The passage is taken from Chavel's Kisvei HaRamban, volume 1, page 142. Once more, we will paraphrase.

תחלת כל דבר יש לך לדעת, שכל מה שהנבראים יודעים ומבינים כלם פירות התורה או פירי פירות שלה, ואלמלא כך אין בין אדם לחמור שהוא רוכב עליו כלום, וכן תראה היום באומות הרחוקות מארץ התורה והנבואה, יושבי הקצוות, כגון יושבי רומ"ניא והת"תרים ואומות צא"בה שאינם מכירים את הבורא וסבורים שהעולם קדמון, וגם אינם מחשבין כלל לא בקדמותו ולא בחדושו, ואם הגלגל מניע עצמו או זולתו מניע, כמו שאמר דוד המלך ע"ה במזמור הזה, וכמו שראו בעלי העיון שלא שמעו התורה, כי האדם בתולדתו בלא מלמד כבהמה שנ' ועיר פרא אדם יולד, ואם דעתו ושכלו של אדם בלא מלמד נותנת לו לחשוב בחדוש, לפי שאין הגלגל מנהיג, אלא זולתו מניע, כמו שהזכרנו, אין אצלו מצוה ולא עבירה, ולא דעת ולא חשבון, ואין אצלו שום מעשה טוב ונרצה יותר מאחר, וכל שכן הימים והשנים שכלם שווים אצלו, נמצא הכל שוה אצלו כמו שהוא שוה אצל הבהמות:

You must realize that, to the extent that you are able to discern wisdom and culture among the gentile nations, this all derives from the fact that they came into contact with the Jews and that, in consequence, the wisdom of the Torah trickled down to them. Once they became aware of the possibilities, they simply adapted whatever suited them to their needs. Without such access to the Torah's wisdom, there is no difference at all between a man and the donkey which is carrying him. You can confirm the truth of what I have said by observing those people who, because of their distance from us, never had any contact with the Torah. . . . Their lives make it clear that man without a teacher is simply another animal. . . . The concept that some actions might be good and therefore ought to be pursued while others are evil and should be shunned is foreign to them. They live their lives in precisely the same mode as animals live theirs.[8]

There we have it. A simple *shidduch* between the Ramban and the Ikarim will get us where we need to get. The Ikarim teaches us that each man is an entire "species"; that no animal has individual worth. Ramban asserts that certain humans fall under the rubric "animal." *Quod erat demonstrandum. Hashgachah*, inasmuch as it covers such humans, is addressed to the group rather than to the individual.

In this chapter we have learned that the two parts of the book, the earlier part dealing with man, the latter with *hashgachah*, are closely linked together. In the Epilogue which now follows, we will learn where all this might lead.

I will quote myself from the Preface which I wrote to this book. Everything follows from that.

I chose to explore Ramban's ideas about the nature of man (chapters 1–10) and of *hashgachah*, God's involvement in human affairs (chapters 11–20). I treated each section as a self-contained unit and did not, as I was researching them, spend much time or thought on how the two might eventually mesh and interact.

That I left for chapter 20 and the Epilogue, which, now that I have written them, seems to me to be the most important part of the book. I did indeed find new dimensions in areas of the Torah which I had long known but never understood as profoundly as I do now. Everyday *mitzvos* sprang to life and were revealed as part of a grand system in which life in the Kingdom of the Ribono shel Olam finds expression.

I meant the strange expression "life in the Kingdom of the Ribono shel Olam" quite literally.[1] I am writing this paragraph on Erev Yom Kippur 5766 and look back upon the nine first days of this year's Aseres Yemei Teshuvah. On Rosh HaShanah we are bound to pronounce the Ribono shel Olam as our king (Rosh HaShanah 16a). In the past I had only the haziest idea of what this really meant in practical terms. I truly believe that having studied the ideas of the Ramban with which I deal in this book and having thought the whole thing through as I laid it down in the Epilogue, I have, to some extent, penetrated to the true meaning of this exercise.

The value of this book stands or falls by what is written here. I believe in it and I hope that so will you. I will give a short background to my thinking and then get to the meat of this Epilogue, the exploration of some simple examples from our civil law which, when I analyzed them in the light of the earlier parts of this book, appeared to me in an entirely new light.

Here is the background.

It has always puzzled me, as I think it has puzzled many people, why *parashas* Mishpatim is wedged in, in the middle of the narrative sections of Shemos. Why was it so important that the people should know these *halachos* at just this particular moment, particularly since many of them—a prime example is *eved Ivri*, the very first of issues with which Mishpatim deals—could have no practical application at that time.[2]

Here is my suggestion for an explanation.

When we came to Sinai, the Ribono shel Olam told us of His plans for us. Through the Torah which He was about to give us, we were to grow into a *mamleches kohanim ve'goy kodosh*, a kingdom of *kohanim* and a holy nation.[3] You will notice that I left the word "*kohanim*" untranslated. I particularly avoided the well-known "Kingdom of Priests" because that does not accord with Rashi's rendering. Rashi claims that *kohanim* here is to be understood as *sarim*, princes or aristocrats. The Ribono shel Olam wanted us to become a kingdom made up of *individuals*, each of high, aristocratic standing. From the context it is clear that a nation made up of such proud *individuals* can grow into a *holy nation*.

Why the stress upon individuality? I think that the answer lies in Shabbos 146a, which teaches that at Sinai, before the tragedy of the *eigel*, Klal Yisrael rose to the standing of Adam HaRishon before he sinned.[4] In the context of all that we have learned in this book, this would mean that for every single man and woman in Israel, the two components which constituted Adam, the animal-like vitality which had already existed before God imbued him with the soul and the soul itself, stood in perfect balance, the one subordinated to the other. Therefore everyone who stood at Sinai qualified as an "individual" in the sense that we defined this term in chapter 20.

That said, it seems to me that the civil laws which are to govern a society made up of God's "aristocrats" would need to reflect this unique standing. Laws which appear straightforward and simple and are applicable to the most ordinary everyday situations will, upon careful analysis, be seen to insist upon standards beyond anything which anyone solely concerned with the smooth running of society would have dreamed.

It is for this reason that Mishpatim occupies the position which it does. In its totality it is a commentary upon our role as *mamleches kohanim ve'goy kodosh*.[5]

It is a heady experience to be part of a kingdom made up of princes and aristocrats. It also makes some very surprising demands. For the rest of this Epilogue we will examine some of the ideas which we are able to uncover.

THE DAF YOMI AND THE KITTEN

Does your confidence in the future of Klal Yisrael ever need a boost? Could you use a little undiluted joy in your life? Here is some failproof advice. Visit your local Yeshiva Ketana and pop in on the fourth or fifth graders struggling with *Has'chalas Gemara*. Here you see the bluest of blue-chip investments in action. These are our treasures which year by year will rise in value though you will never see them listed on the tip sheets which clog up your e-mail. There is nothing quite like the feeling of gratitude which will well up inside you when you are privileged to observe living, pulsating *nishmas Yisrael* up close.

The odds are that the children will be studying *Eilu Metzios,* the section in Bava Metzia which deals with the *mitzvah* of returning a lost object to its owner. I do not know when it became customary to choose just this section to introduce the children to the rigors of Gemara learning, but certainly today it is very widespread.[6]

Let us then join the class and find out what the Torah expects of us. It all sounds pretty simple. I am playing in the schoolyard and find Yankel's wallet. I pick it up, bring it to him and the case is closed. I have chalked up another merit in my *mitzvah* column. If the Rebbi saw what was happening he will send home a note to tell my parents what a fine Ben Torah I have shown myself to be.

What could be simpler?

Let us consider the following case.

I am a professional, working hard to support my family. The highlight of my day is the Daf Yomi which I attend at night and I allow nothing, *but nothing at all*, to get in the way of my attendance. I don't go to weddings, I don't go to meetings, I don't go to banquets. I even skipped my daughter's graduation.[7] The Daf is the Daf is the Daf.

Very well. I have gulped down my supper, patted the children on the head, thanked my wife for the thousandth time for helping them with their homework and for being unremittingly understanding and encouraging of my learning,[8] and I am on my way. I am about to get into my car, when I hear a mewing sound in the distance. Intrigued, I look up and see a cat, clearly lost, coming down the street.

What does the Ribono shel Olam now want from me and how does He want me to deal with my Daf Yomi shiur?

Quite simply, He insists that I forget about the Daf and more or less let the cat take over my life. I have no idea who the owner might be, but it is now my obligation to find out.

Clearly I cannot leave the cat outside. It would simply wander off. So, for starters, I have to pick it up (I have never *touched* a cat in my life!) and take it inside. Even before I begin to feed it (clearly, if I am going to make sure that it is returned to its owner, I cannot let it starve). I notice a cut on its leg which, unattended, might become gangrenous. This clearly calls for a vet. (A *vet* at nine o'clock in the evening!?) By the time I have bedded down the little kitten in my living room it is midnight. I flop into bed, mindful of the fact that it will require another feeding in the morning. And so on and on and on, perhaps for several weeks, until I will have been able to find the owner.[9]

What are the conceptual underpinnings of this *halachah*? How are we to understand why the Torah would impose such unimaginable inconvenience upon perfectly innocent people, simply in order to facilitate the return of a silly little cat to its owner?

To the best of my knowledge there are no equivalent obligations under any secular system of law with which I am at all familiar. At the most, a finder might be forbidden to appropriate a lost object for himself; I am not even sure of that, but there is certainly no legal expectation that he go out of his way to find the owner and make sure that he recovers his property. What do these seemingly unreasonable demands tell us about ourselves and our society?

It seems to me that for a real understanding we will have to invoke Yaakov Avinu and the famous *pachim ketanim*, the small kitchen utensils for the recovery of which he risked his life by remaining alone and unprotected by the river (Chulin 91a).[10] Why did he do this? What can be so important about a bunch of small kitchen tools?[11] The Gemara offers an explanation: *Tzadikim*, who never ever would dream of taking anything that is not their own, value there possessions more than they value their own bodies. Yaakov Avinu knew that he had not stolen those implements. God had given them to him. Clearly the Ribono shel Olam must have had some purpose in making sure that he had them. He had no right to treat them cavalierly.

The Torah obliges me to look upon my neighbor's property as Yaakov looked upon his own. The kitten, or whatever else the man may have lost, might not seem very important to me. Certainly not to the extent that I should feel obliged to sacrifice a considerable chunk of my life to facilitate its return. But the Ribono shel Olam asks just that of me. The owner of the cat is a prince. God blew some of His own essence into his body. His physical world is altogether subordinate to that soul. So every part of that physical world has something to contribute to his full service of God. *Pachim ketanim* may appear "small" (*ketanim*) to you, but they have a greatness all of their own hidden within their modest dimensions. Return them to your brother!

The obligation to return a lost object takes on an entirely new coloration, does it not?

There is another subject which I would like to visit. It is *hashmatas kesafim*, the canceling of debts at the end of the *shmitah* year. Torah law prescribes that all debts are automatically forgiven at the end of the seven-year cycle which culminates in the *shmitah* year.[12]

FORGIVING DEBTS

It is generally assumed that the Ribono shel Olam instituted *hashmatas kesafim* as a kind of welfare program for the poor.[13] As much as creditors should be able to collect what is owed them, the poor must also be protected from crushing indebtedness. In a society based upon agriculture the need for relief would be especially urgent at the end of the *shmitah* year when there is no harvest which could be converted into cash with which to meet obligations.

Now Gittin 36b records that Hillel propagated the ordinance of *pruzbul*. Creditors would be able to execute a legal instrument which would vest the right to collect their debt in the courts. The creditor himself would henceforth be out of the picture. If he was involved at all, it would be as an agent of the court. Once the debt was collected by the courts, they would restore the money to the original creditor.[14]

Hillel undertook to effectively emasculate the law of *hashmatas kesafim* because he observed that people were finding it harder and harder to borrow money. Potential lenders simply stopped extending credit when the *shmitah* year was approaching. In doing so they violated Torah law (Devarim 15:9) which specifically forbids such fiscal prudence.[15] Something needed to be done, and Hillel did it.

The need for the ordinance was obviously real. Nevertheless, Hillel's solution seems radical indeed. Beis Din's ability to pass ordinances is generally used to *augment* the law,[16] not to circumvent it. With *pruzbul* in place, few loans indeed would ever be subject to *hashmatas kesafim*. Was Hillel not simply frustrating the will of the Ribono shel Olam?

It is my belief that a careful analysis of Devarim 15:1–6 will yield a different rational for *hashmatas kesafim*.

א. מקץ שבע שנים תעשה שמטה.

ב. וזה דבר השמטה שמוט כל בעל משה ידו אשר ישה ברעהו לא יגש את רעהו ואת אחיו כי קרא שמטה ליהוה.

ג. את הנכרי תגוש ואת אשר יהיה לך את אחיך לא תגוש.

ד. אפס כי לא יהיה בך אביון כי ברך יברכך יהוה בארץ אשר יהוה אלהיך נתן לך נחלה לרשתה.

ה. רק אם שמוע תשמע בקול יהוה אלהיך לשמר לעשות את כל המצוה הזאת אשר אנכי מצוך היום.

ו. כי יהוה אלהיך ברכך כאשר דבר לך והעבטת גוים רבים ואתה לא תעבט ומשלת בגוים רבים ובך לא ימשלו.

1. As the seven years come to a close, you shall celebrate the *shmitah*.

2. This is the obligation which the *shmitah* imposes upon you: Let every "master of the obligation which his hand imposed" withdraw his claim upon that for which his debtor is indebted to him. He shall make no claims against his fellow, his brother, for he has declared a *shmitah* year to God.

3. Do press your claims upon a stranger but from claims which you have upon your brother you must withdraw.

4. However, you will find that there are no indigents among you, for HaShem will bless you in the land which He has given to you as an inheritance to inherit it.

5. However, all this is provided that you listen to the voice of HaShem your God, to obey in every way the commandments which I command you this day.

6. For HaShem your God has blessed you in accordance with His promise such that you will take pledges from many nations, but they will not take pledges from you, and you will rule over many nations, but they will not rule over you.

I have claimed that a careful reading of this passage will reveal that the rational for *hashmatas kesafim* is something other than the wish to make life a little easier for the debtor. I will argue that, in the spirit of Mishlei 22:7, *The rich rule the poor, and the borrower is the slave of the lender.*[17] The remission of debts seeks to limit the extent of the mastery which the creditor exercises over the debtor. It redounds to the benefit of the "master" as much as to the benefit of the "slave." If it is painful and humiliating to be in the control of another, it is unhealthy and debilitating to hold one's fellow in thrall.

Now, clearly, I will have to back up this assertion with some solid evidence. I will offer three types of argument: (1) an analysis of the language in which the law of *hashmatas kesafim* is couched; (2) an examination of the promises which the Torah makes as a reward for the conscientious fulfillment of this command; and (3) a look at the context in which this *mitzvah* appears. The *parshios* which immediately precede and follow this one will point us in the right direction.

1. The language: the analysis of the language is going to be rather technical. Not all of you may be interested in these fine points of grammar and usage so I will shift this section into an Appendix to this Epilogue. It will be there for you if you want it; you need not feel guilty if you decide to skip it.

But even here we can draw attention to a textual oddity though we will leave the details to the Appendix. If you will glance at the translation which I offered for verse 2, you will see an absolutely awful circumlocution for the simple word "creditor," which, so it seems, would have served as well.[18] The phrase as it appears there is "master of the obligation which his hand has imposed." Why the pedantically literal "master" for *baal*? Why "obligation" for *mashei* which could just as well be rendered "loan"? And why translate *yado*, "hand," when *mashei yado* seems so obviously to be idiomatic—we all know that idioms ought *never* to be taken literally?[19]

By now the thrust of my argument should be clear. There is a perfectly good Hebrew word for "creditor" which is used throughout TaNaCh. It is *Noshé* (see Shemos 22:24, II Melachim 4:1, Yeshaya 3:1 and elsewhere). Nowhere else do we find *baal mashei yado*. I believe that this strange usage clearly indicates the theory which I am suggesting. It looks upon the creditor as one who is exercising mastery over another.[20]

2. The promises: Verse 6 offers two rewards for conscientious fulfillment of the *hashmatas kesafim* requirement. The first promises self-sufficiency. We would be in the position of making loans to others, but we would not need to contract loans. That is logical enough. It seems appropriate to reward a creditor who behaved magnanimously to his hapless debtor by guaranteeing that he himself would never find himself in that unfortunate position.

On the face of it, the second promise is less easy to understand. Why should adherence to the requirement of *hashmatas kesafim* be rewarded by making us rulers over other nations and by guaranteeing that others will never rule over us? Of course, if our theory is correct, everything becomes very simple. *Hashmatas kesafim* is designed to impose limits upon the degree to which we are able to exercise mastery over our debtors. In the merit of allowing our own legitimate mastery to be curbed we are promised that no one else will ever lord it over us.

3. The context: The *parashah* of *hashmatas kesafim* is preceded by the one dealing with *maaser sheini*[21] and *maaser ani*[22] and is followed by the one dealing with the *haanakah*[23] of an *eved Ivri*.[24]

The short survey which I am about to give concerning *maaser sheini* and *maaser ani* is based upon the writings of Rav Dovid Tzvi Hoffman in his commentary to Devarim. Of course nothing can replace the satisfaction which comes from actually studying his ideas in detail from the original. If any of you, dear Readers, can summon up the time and energy to do so, I highly recommend that you do so. Within the time and space constraints to which this essay must adhere I can only adumbrate what is offered there.

For those of you who are not really familiar with the ideas of *terumah, maaser rishon, maaser sheini* and *maaser ani*, I recommend that you take another brief look at note 21.

Terumah and *maaser rishon* are given to the *kohen* and *levi* respectively in recognition of the farmer's understanding that the harvest stored in his silos comes to him from the Ribono shel Olam. They might be viewed as a kind of tax which upon payment frees the harvest for the owner's use.

What then is *maaser sheini*? The farmer has already paid his dues. What else does the Torah want from him? Its function is to bring home to the farmer that even after the harvest is legally his to use, it still must be enjoyed in a holy manner. Ideally it would be consumed in Yerushalayim, a city saturated with sanctity. Since that is patently impossible for people living all over Eretz Yisrael, we are enjoined to eat at least the first tenth there.

That given, we need to do some thinking about the *maaser ani* which replaces the *maaser sheini* in the third and sixth years of the *shmitah* cycle. What does filling the needs of an indigent have to do with sanctity? The conclusion which we must draw is inevitable. *Maaser ani* is not like other charity. It does not begin with the indigent's need for help but with the donor's need to *give* help. It is part of holiness to be caring and giving. To invest our eating with sanctity, we need to go to Yerushalayim. To *be* holy, it is enough to open our eyes and hearts to another.

For our purpose in this essay we might sum up as follows. The advantage which the indigent draws from the *maaser ani* which he receives is coincidental. The rational for this *mitzvah* is located in the giver's need to be trained in holy living.

We now move on to *haanakah,* the severance gift which the owner must give to an *eved Ivri* when he sets him free. It is discussed in the *parashah* which immediately follows the one which deals with *hashmatas kesafim.*

We have no need to analyze the passage in detail. A correct understanding of the unusual verb which the Torah uses, *ha'aneik ta'anik,*[25] will tell us what we need to know. The verb *anok*, with the meaning of *gifting* which it carries here, does not recur in TaNaCh so there is very little help in unraveling the particular shade of meaning which it conveys. Ibn Ezra refers us to the noun *anak*[26] which means a necklace or a pendant hanging as an ornament from the neck. Hence we have the sense *"bedeck him with jewelry"* by showering him with severance gifts. This phrase, Ibn Ezra feels, can mean only that it is incumbent upon the owner to send his former slave away with honor. I understand this to mean that the former slave is to be helped over his embarrassing past. History is, so to speak, erased. The gift which the master renders him in spite of the fact that he had already paid in full for his services marks him as an honored worker rather than a lowly slave.

Have you caught the commonality? In the case of both *haanakah* and *hashmatas kesafim* someone benefits from another's generosity—in the one case through having his debt forgiven, in the other through being showered with gifts. Yet in both cases it is not this benefit which motivates the *mitzvah. Haanakah* is meant to restore dignity to a former slave; *hashmatas kesafim* wishes to establish boundaries to the extent to which a lender can be master over a needy borrower. If we now recall what we demonstrated about the nature of *maaser ani*, we can see that it also fits smoothly into this set. There, the tithe given to the poor beggar obviously benefits him, but it is not for that reason that the farmer is obliged to give it. Rather it is in order that the giver may be educated into living a life of sanctity.

I feel that I have delivered on my undertaking to provide solid backing for the theory which I propounded above concerning the purpose of *hashmatas kesafim*.

That done, we can return to the misgivings which we expressed concerning Hillel's ordinance. Obviously, we had no quarrel with the legality of the new system. The poor needed help obtaining credit as the *shmitah* year approached. Hillel had the power to ordain *pruzbul* legislation. Still, so it seemed to us, the ordinance *does* seem to clash head-on with the Torah.

The problem is solved if our explanation is correct. It is the lording of one Jew over another which the Torah is seeking to rein in. That lording is eliminated even if the debt remains collectible through the execution of a *pruzbul*. Recall that the efficacy of the *pruzbul* is predicated upon Beis Din assuming the right to collect the debt. Remember that the creditor himself loses any right he had to force payment of the loan. Indeed his mastery over the hapless debtor has effectively been eliminated. The Torah law has not been circumvented at all.

We headed this section "Life Among God's '*Chasidim*.'" We wanted to make the point that a society made up of those who live as the Ribono shel Olam intended us to live, in whom the "animal" remains always subordinated to the *nefesh chayah*, can make demands upon the individual. For such a society, the fabric of everyday living can be made infinitely richer. The marketplace can become another Beis HaMidrash, kittens can become offerings brought on the altar of a worldview which puts things into their right perspective, and the cold legalities of an ownership bereft of human feelings can morph into a nuanced guardianship which is responsive to interpersonal human values of which the law books know nothing at all.

Epilogue

I suppose that I could, that perhaps I should, end here. Still, I feel so overwhelmed by the discovery which I have made and which I have shared with you in this essay that I have decided on a little self-indulgence. Here is my excuse. This Epilogue has asked a lot of you, dear Reader. It is long and in many ways, hard reading, in much the same way as it has been long and in many ways, hard, writing. If you have made it to this point, it must be that you, like I, have become intoxicated by the sheer excitement of the chase. It is a heady experience to feel that we are on the track of something valuable, that we have perhaps chanced upon a closer acquaintance with the way Ramban looked upon the world.

Let us turn to the prohibition against *ribbis*, lending money against interest. Now we are not dealing with usury where exorbitant, bloodsucking interest is charged to desperate people. No enlightened society would tolerate such evil. But why should "renting" out my money for a reasonable return be interdicted any more than renting out my apartment or my car? Yet, it is forbidden, even to the extent that the debtor may not give his lender a cheerful "Good morning" if he does so only in recognition of the favor which he received at the lender's hand (Yoreh De'ah 160:11).

Moreover, Yoreh De'ah 160:2 tells us that a person who lends out his money against *ribbis* is thereby "denying" our redemption from Egypt and shrugging off Israel's God. Where does Egypt come into all this?

It all sounds a little exaggerated, does it not, particularly when applied to a practice that seems entirely consonant with decency and consideration.

Let us take a look at the passage in Shemos 22:24 and then study Ramban's remarks.

> When you lend money to My people, to the poor amongst you, do not act towards him as would a creditor. Do not impose interest upon him.[27]

Immediately there is a flashing yellow light. Why My *people* when the phrase immediately afterwards, *do not act towards* HIM, indicates clearly that we are referring to an individual borrower. I cannot swear to this, but as much as I can be certain, there is not a single other instance in which the Torah uses *ami*, My people, when it refers to an individual.

It seems clear that this unusual language is meant to set the stage for what is to follow. It is designed to anticipate the very question which has troubled us so much. It is as though the Ribono shel Olam is saying to us, "I know that what I am about to ask of you is going to seem unreasonable. I am going to request that you forgo what any prudent person would do as a matter of course. I want you to take what would naturally be regarded as a normal business transaction and drain it of any association with business. Take your hard-earned money and lend it as a gesture of love. The man needs it, you have it, both of you are a part of My beloved people. You were slaves together, you were freed together, you must live together and you must love together. I brought you out of Egypt to make you Mine. I am entitled to demand that you understand."

As I have taken it, *ami* here is a kind of aside addressed to the lender. It is designed to persuade him to comply to a demand which may not be difficult in itself but nevertheless militates against all logic as he, the lender, might see it. In this it would precisely parallel the next verse where the Ribono shel Olam also finds it necessary to persuade a lender to go along with an obligation which would seem utterly outlandish to him. We read: *If you take your neighbor's garment as a security, you must return it to him before sunset. This alone is his covering, the garment for his skin.* WITH WHAT WOULD HE SLEEP? . . . Here too the Torah tugs at the heart of the lender. It is as though the Ribono shel Olam is saying, "I know quite well that a blanket that you must bring to the borrower's home every night or must, at least, surrender to him is not going to be much of a pledge. He will be more secure in the knowledge that he can anticipate a comfortable night's sleep than you are that you will see your money back. I know. I know. But, do you have an answer to My question? Can you live with yourself knowing that he is shivering in his frigid room? Bring him back his pledge. It may not make sense to the mind, but the heart understands."

Ramban understood the profundity of what the Torah demands

from every simple Jew who happens to have a few extra dollars which he is willing to lend out to a fellow Jew.

לא תהיה לו כנושה הוא המלוה, יאמר שלא תהיה לו כמלוה שהוא כמושל ללוה כענין שכתוב ועבד לוה לאיש מלוה (משלי כב ז), אבל תהיה לו בכל דבר כאלו לא לוה ממך לעולם, ולא תשים עליו נשך, שהוא נשך כסף נשך אוכל (דברים כג כ), אבל תהיה ההלואה אליו חסד, לא תטול ממנו תועלת כבוד ולא תועלת ממון:

The Torah is addressing the lender, exhorting him that he should not act towards the borrower as a creditor, that is, as Mishlei 22:7 makes clear, a master who rules over his servant. He is to act towards the lender as though he had never lent him any money at all. He is not to charge any interest which would give the transaction the nature of a business deal. Rather, it is to be an act of undiluted kindness. The lender is not to derive any benefit from the loan, not money and not honor.

Ramban to Devarim 23:20 expands on the same issue:

הרבית שהוא נעשה לדעת שניהם וברצונם לא נאסר אלא מצד האחוה והחסד, כמו שצוה (ויקרא יט יח) ואהבת לרעך כמוך, וכמו שאמר (לעיל טו ט) השמר לך פן יהיה דבר עם לבבך בליעל וגו' , ועל כן אמר למען יברכך ה' אלהיך, כי חסד ורחמים יעשה עם אחיו כאשר ילונו בלא רבית ותחשב לו לצדקה וכן השמיטה חסד באחים, לכך אמר (שם פסוק ג) את הנכרי תגוש, וקבע לו ברכה, כי הכתוב לא יזכיר הברכה רק בצדקה ובחסדים, לא בגזל ובגנבה ובאונאה:

Here is a paraphrase.

Only the Ribono shel Olam's wish that relationships between Jews should be governed by kindness and brotherly love can explain why the Torah would forbid the levying of interest which, quite possibly, the borrower would be happy to pay in order to secure a loan. This prohibition is of a piece with the command that we love our neighbors as we love ourselves. It falls into the same category as the prohibition against withholding a loan because of the imminence of the *shmitah* year.

In neither case could the lender's prudent concern for the preservation of his wealth be labeled as evil. Still, the Ribono shel Olam is not satisfied by a correct relationship in which business is business. He wants a people who deal with each other with kindness and with mercy. These dictate making loans without interest and with a willingness to run the risk that they will likely be abrogated in the *shmitah*.

We have reached the end of our ruminations. It is not that we have run out of material but that a thorough analysis of the entire corpus of civil law in *halachah* would require a book all to itself. Shlomo HaMelech (Mishlei 9:9) has taught us that offering the wise the beginnings of a thesis is enough. After that, they will carry the ball on their own.

והדרך צלח רכב על דבר אמת וענוה צדק ותורך נוראות ימינך.

In your glory, win success! Ride on in the cause of truth and meekness and right! Let your right hand lead you to awesome deeds! (Tehilim 45:5).[28]

May the Ribono shel Olam speed you on your way.

APPENDIX TO CHAPTER 3

*H*erewith an excerpt from my book, *Beginnings*, which deals with topics from *parashas* Bereishis. It considers Rashi's comments to Bereishis 2:3.

... אשר ברא אלהים לעשות. המלאכה שהיתה ראויה לעשות בשבת, כפל ועשאה בששי, כמו שמפורש בבראשית רבה.

[The phrase is to be understood that] ... God created [on the sixth day] what should really have been left for Shabbos (Bereishis Rabbah 1:9).

The assertion that some of what was made on Friday should have been left for Shabbos is fascinating. It compels us to wonder which of Friday's creations these might be. Furthermore, we must try to understand why they should have been left for Shabbos and why, given that assumption, they were pushed forward to Friday.[1] We have here a small Rashi with many profound implications.

It seems obvious that man is the standout. He, the צלם אלהים, is out of place among the animals. We would certainly have expected that he be assigned to a different day.

However, more than simply a day of his own is at stake. The Midrash speaks of a מלאכה שהיתה ראויה לעשות בשבת. Let us postulate that we have guessed correctly and that it is man who is meant. In what sense would Shabbos have been the ideal day for him to be created?

Because then, so it appears to me, man created on Shabbos would have been the "Shabbosdicker Yid," who is the focus of our dreams and our strivings. Had this happened, then the first six days would have been linked to Shabbos as preparation is linked to fulfillment, as the subordinate is to purpose and goal. The instrumental nature of the physical world would have been clearly spelled out. We would not have required R' Yaakov (Avos 4:16) to tell us that העולם הזה דומה לפרוזדור בפני העולם הבא, *This world can*

117

be described as an antechamber leading into the next. History itself would have made this clear.

But the Ribono shel Olam had other plans. By making man on Friday and not on Shabbos, God placed him squarely into a flawed world, one fraught for him with pitfalls and dangers, with zigs and zags, with times of heady progress vying with those of devastating failures. Shabbos, far from being his natural environment, becomes a prize towards which he has to claw and fight his way, ever onwards, ever upwards.

"המלאכה שהיתה ראויה לעשות" means that that is what would have happened in an ideal world. However, the Ribono shel Olam did not want to make such an ideal world on His own. He wanted to involve humanity in attaining it. We were to become His partners in finding perfection. Adam was created on Friday, together with the animals. He would have to make his own way to Shabbos.

*T*his Appendix is not for the fainthearted. We are going to get a little technical, and there may be some of you who tend to feel threatened when faced with the complexities of *dikduk*. Still, what I have to say here is, in my opinion, very important indeed, and I feel pretty certain that, if you stick with me, you will rewarded in the end by being able to translate one of the most difficult verses in the Torah with satisfying clarity.

I apologize to those of you who do not read Hebrew. The subject of this essay is such that the use of Hebrew can simply not be avoided.

Here is the text which we are going to examine. Unlike the usual quotes which we have used throughout this book, we will display the vowels, since these will play a significant role in our analysis. The quote comes from Devarim 15:1–3.

א. מִקֵּץ שֶׁבַע שָׁנִים תַּעֲשֶׂה שְׁמִטָּה.

ב. וְזֶה דְּבַר הַשְּׁמִטָּה שָׁמוֹט כָּל בַּעַל מַשֵּׁה יָדוֹ אֲשֶׁר יַשֶּׁה בְּרֵעֵהוּ לֹא יִגֹּשׂ אֶת רֵעֵהוּ וְאֶת אָחִיו כִּי קָרָא שְׁמִטָּה לַיהֹוָה.

ג. אֶת הַנָּכְרִי תִּגֹּשׂ וַאֲשֶׁר יִהְיֶה לְךָ אֶת אָחִיךָ תַּשְׁמֵט יָדֶךָ.

1. At the end of every seven years, you shall celebrate the *shmitah*.

2. The idea of the *shmitah* is that every creditor shall remit any debt owed by his neighbor and brother because a *shmitah* year has been pronounced for God.

3. You may collect money from the alien, but if you have any claim against your brother, you must relinquish it.

I have used the translation of the late Rabbi Aryeh Kaplan in *The Living Torah*, because it is specific enough to convey the meaning of the verses, but not so literal that it has to take sides in the issues which we will have to discuss. We have a clear field in which to parade the questions which have to be solved.

We will first consider verse 2 and then draw on verse 3 to support our conclusions. For verse 2 we will first present Rashi's interpretation and point out that, firstly, it does not accord with Targum, and secondly, it poses a number of stylistic and grammatical difficulties. Taking Targum as our base, we will then present an alternative to Rashi's interpretation and draw conclusions from it. Much of our analysis of Rashi is taken from R. Dovid Tzvi Hoffman's Commentary to Devarim.

Let us then turn our attention to verse 2 and try to untangle the following words: שמוט כל בעל משה ידו אשר ישה נרעהו. Where do the commas go? Who is the subject and what the object in this sentence.

We will first get the word "שָׁמוֹט", out of the way. The *komatz* under the *shin* marks it as the infinitive form of שמט. As often happens, the infinitive is used instead of the regular imperative which should be שְׁמוֹט. This is in no way unusual and need not detain us any longer.

So we have a command addressed to someone to *let go*. Who is being commanded and from what is he to distance himself? Who is the subject and what is the object?

Rashi appears to take "ידו" as the object and "כל בעל משה" as the subject.[1] Every "*baal masheh*" is to withdraw his hand. According to some readings in Rashi, he proves this from verse 3 where we have תשמט ידיך, which, if we take תשמט as the second person masculine in the future tense,[2] could be translated as *you shall withdraw your hand.*

Rashi is silent on the last few words in verse 2, אשר ישה ברעהו. If we simply translate the words for what they say, we would have to render, *who lent money to his neighbor.* It would be a modifier for בעל משה, the subject. Taken together it would read . . . בעל משה אשר ישה ברעהו, *Every creditor . . . who lent money to his neighbor.* The second phrase certainly appears to be redundant. What does אשר ישה ברעהו add to בעל משה?

Then there is the spelling of מַשֶּׁה. The word belongs to the same family as מַטֶּה, *a staff.* Now in the construct form (סמיכות), the *segol* in מַטֶּה changes to a *tzeireh*, מַטֵּה הָאֱלֹהִים, *God's staff* (Shemos 4:18). משה in our verse is written with a *tzeireh,* and we must conclude that it is in the construct form and joined to ידו, *the* MASHEH *of his hand.* This reading precludes the possibility of taking ידו as the object of בעל משה. The *trop* too, which places a *zakef katan* on ידו, is clearly joining ידו to משה.

Then there is the matter of תשמט ידו in verse 3. As we pointed out in note 2, it is in the *hiphil,* תַּשְׁמֵט instead of תִּשְׁמוֹט. As Rashi takes the phrase, there seems no logic to the change from the *kal* in verse 2 to the *hiphil* in verse 3.

Finally we note that in the language of the Gemara, the object of שמט is the land or the debt which must be relinquished. Thus, in Gittin 36a, בזמן שאתה משמט קרקע אתה משמט כספים. Rashi's use of ידו as the object of שמט is postulating that Chazal used שמט differently from the way it is used in the Torah.

All these difficulties are solved if we take all three words, בעל משה ידו, as the subject of the sentence, and אשר ישה ברעהו as the object. *Let the creditor, the* בעל משה ידו, *forgive that of his neighbor over which he has a claim,* אשר ישה ברעהו.

This is clearly Targum's rendering. He has, ... דישמט כל גבר מרי ישו דירשי בחבריה. The ד in דירשי, THAT WHICH HE IS OWED, makes clear that that is where the object begins and that what comes before, כל גבר מריה רשו, is the subject.[3]

Once all this is established, we would need to ask ourselves why a simple creditor, to whom the Torah in all other places refers to as the נשה (see Shemos 22:24 and all similar passages), should here be called a בעל משה ידו, which translates as *one who is master* (בעל) *of a debt* (משה) *which is a mark of his power* (ידו), taking the hand as a synonym for power as, for example, in Shemos 14:31.

It seems quite clear that this confirms the thesis which we propounded in the Epilogue. *Hashmatas kesafim* is not, in the first instance, a means of helping the poor by canceling their debts, but a way of curbing the power which a creditor exercises over his debtor. On reflection we can confirm this from verse 3 where we have תַּשְׁ־מֵט יָדֶךָ in the *hiphil* instead of תִּשְׁמוֹט in the *kal.* The meaning is:

Make your hand (i.e., your power) curb itself. Do not allow your mastery free rein.

It is as I claimed. A careful reading of the *parashah* yields precisely what we worked out in the Epilogue.[4]

NOTES

PREFACE

1. ובאמת הספר הזה הוא יסוד אמונה ושרש הדת. I am not particularly proud of the paraphrase which I offer within. After much thought, it is the best that I can offer at the moment.

2. תורה עם פי' רמב"ן תהגו ותלמדו עם בניכם, כי הוא ראש אמונת אומן, ובו תחכמו מכלכל דרדע והימן.

3. אבל מה אעשה ונפשי חשקה בתורה, והיא בלבי כאש אוכלת בוערה, בכליותי עצורה (Introduction to the Commentary).

4. להניח דעת התלמידים, ייגיעי הגלות והצרות (Introduction to Bereishis).

5. לצאת בעקבי הראשונים אריות שבחבורה (Introduction to the Torah).

1: WORKING MIRACLES

1. This is true of most of the dictionaries which I consulted. I came across some which do have *to purify spiritually*. However, they limit this translation to scriptural usage and we are striving towards a translation for everyday English.

2. See, for example, Tehilim 118:10.

3. ומלתם את ערלת לבבכם.

4. As we saw from Ramban, this is not really a renewal at all. It signifies a return to Eden.

5. Ramban himself seems to answer this question by interpreting the phrase *circumcise your heart* as שיהיה לבבכם פתוח לדעת האמת, *that your hearts might be open to understand the truth*. This certainly is something very much less powerful than the picture which he draws for us in Nitzavim.

Of course, that itself requires an explanation. What permitted Ramban to throw consistency to the winds? We will be discussing this Ramban in chapter 10, where we will bring this section of the book to a close.

6. יסוד ההסידות ושורש העבודה התמימה.

7. שיתברר.

8. ויתאמת.

9. מה חובתו בעולמו.

2: BACK TO THE BEGINNINGS

1. The concept that when two things come very close to each other, they could be seen as "kissing" is based upon Tehilim 85:11; see commentators there. The term is used in Rabbinic Hebrew where in certain situations two bodies of water are brought into contact with each other through a manner described as השקה from נשק, *to kiss*.

I have used this evocative term intentionally. As we trace Ramban's view of man throughout the following essays, we will discover the degree to which the two disparate units, heaven and earth, can meet and blend in complex man.

2. נעשה אדם בצלמנו כדמותנו.

3. We cannot explain נעשה as constituting the royal plural since, throughout the

Torah, God speaks of Himself in the singular. Thus, *I am HaShem your God . . .* in the Asseres HaDibros.

4. See chapter 5 for more detail.

5. I have used the words "miraculously" and "created" purposefully. I will elaborate on this in the next chapter.

3: CREATING MAN

1. It is very obvious that we understand very little of what the Torah tells us concerning the six days of Creation. Ramban himself, at Bereishis 1:1, notes that *none of it can really be known clearly*. Still, we certainly intuit that, to the extent that the six "days" mean anything at all to us, they stand for discrete stages of coming into being and that therefore the various groupings which were called into existence upon any particular "day" had a close affinity to one another.

2. See Appendix to this chapter.

3. I have used the word "image" here, as a temporary measure. Later on in this essay, I will provide a more nuanced description for the meaning of צלם.

4. A word about the Ramban's use of היולי and the English forms of this word which I have used throughout this essay. Ramban defines it as דק מאד שאין בו ממש, *something which is extremely "thin" and has no substance.*

In Greek *hyle* means *material*. Examples of modern usage confirm this translation: *hylicism* for materialism and hylogenesis for the origin of matter.

Now the word דק implies that there is some material, but that it is very "thin." That is how both the Torah and Ramban in his commentary use the word in Shemos 14 when describing the *mon*. That given, we will not be able to take אין בו ממש literally. It must be, it is so "thin" that, for practical purposes it is as good as nonexistent.

It has been suggested, and I believe that there is a great deal that speaks for this interpretation, that the *hyle* is the atom. Now atoms certainly are material. The word is formed from the Greek *a* meaning "not," and *tomos*, "to split." That is, it describes the smallest possible material, so small that it cannot be divided (the belief at that time). Since atoms are the building blocks of everything in the Universe, they actually provide what Ramban claims to be the function of the *hyle*. As we know, atoms are very small. According to an encyclopedia which I have handy, a drop of water contains 100 billion billion of them. We can sleep at night knowing that Rambam would use אין בו ממש to describe something so minuscule.

A further possibility which could justify the use of אין בו ממש to describe the atom is that, in fact, most of the atom is space. At the center is the nucleus that is surrounded by vast space (in atomic terms) in which the electrons orbit.

My apologies to people who know something about science, for my rather bumbling lay efforts. It may not hold up so well in the laboratory, but it is accurate enough for our purpose here.

5. I am concentrating on צלם because דמות means, very simply, "similarity." Ramban says quite clearly, כי הקרובים בענין, יקראו דומים זה לזה (1:26). Moreover, Ramban spelled out precisely in which way man is דומה both to the earth and the עליונים in the piece which I quoted earlier in this chapter. He will be similar to the earth from which he was produced in the way that his body is constructed, but, through his *ru'ach* (רוח) being incorporeal and immortal he will resemble the creatures of the upper realms.

6. Ramban, in fact, feels it necessary to explain what the function of the verse is.

Why tell us that God created man in "His" Godly צלם without mentioning that He also created him in the earthly צלם. His answer is that the function of this verse is לספר הפלא אשר נפלא בו משאר הנבראים, to inform us of man's uniqueness. In all of Creation there is nothing quite like him.

4: A KISS THAT CAN CHANGE A LIFE

1. I just took my own advice and thought about kissing. I wondered whether animals kiss. My not particularly far-ranging research yielded that kissing, or something very like it, is very much a part of the social life of various animals. In terms of the issues of these essays, kissing is a function of the life force rather than of the soul.

2. שפתים ישק משיב דברים נכחים.

3. See also Bereishis 41:40, ועל פיך ישק כל עמי. There are those who derive ישק from נשק, "to kiss" (see Ibn Ezra and his various commentators). Karnei Ohr cites Ibn Ganach, the grammarian, who explains, "Just as the lips of people kissing each other are pressed closely together, so too the people of Mitzrayim will adhere closely to your wishes."

4. וקרב אתם אחד אל אחד לך לעץ אחד והיו לאחדים בידך.

5. השקה, from the root נשק, "to kiss."

6. וחי בהם.

5: THE "*LAMED*" TELLS A STORY

1. וייצר ה' אלהים את האדם עפר מן האדמה ויפח באפיו נשמת חיים ויהי האדם לנפש חיה.

2. לנפש חיה.

3. נפש חיתא.

4. לרוח ממללא.

5. For example, ובא לציון גואל.

6. For example, לה' הארץ ומלואה.

7. One particularly interesting example is: *lamed* can replace את, which indicates a direct object. Thus, ואהבת לרעך כמוך, in contrast to ואהבת את ה' אלהיך. See Ramban, VaYikra 19:18, who builds an entire philosophy of human relationships on the basis of this change.

8. This is the option which, as Ramban sees it, is yielded by the simple meaning of the verse. It is the one which he examines before he moves on to the Targum's rendering of *nefesh chayah*.

9. This is Ramban's first interpretation of the Targum's rendering of the text.

10. In his commentary to verse 14 he demonstrates this from various expressions which the Torah uses. We have a statement that the *nefesh* (the term which Ramban here uses for life force) is "in" the blood; another statement that the blood is "in" the *nefesh,* and a third, that the blood "is" the *nefesh.* Clearly, then, there is an absolute identity between the two.

6: THE GARDEN OF EDEN I

1. I am not absolutely sure that there were animals in the Garden. There are commentators who interpret God's charge to Adam that he was to cultivate and *guard* the garden (Bereishis 2:15) to mean that he was to keep the animals out so that they would not somehow damage the trees. Still, since the *nachash*, the snake, was clearly there, it seems likely that there were also other animals.

2. This translation follows Ramban. Rashi takes מקדם as, *in the eastern part of Eden.*

3. ויטע יקוק אלהים **גן בעדן** מקדם וישם שם את האדם אשר יצר.

4. These are not the actual words of Radak. He speaks only of the body luxuriating in the Garden's tangible gifts and the soul luxuriating in an inner, hidden something which he does not identify. I have expanded his words here in a direction which, I believe, inheres in the story as it is told to us.

7: THE GARDEN OF EDEN II

1. See 1:28–32. The context makes clear that this command was pronounced later when Chavah had already been created (see Rashi in his second interpretation).

2. חובות הלבבות.

3. See Sanhedrin 56b, which interprets the verse which we are discussing as hinting at the Seven Noachide Laws. However, since the Torah reveals this to us at the level of דרש rather than at the level of פשט, we may conclude that this story at the פשט level which concerns us here wishes us to understand what is being said in the way in which we have presented it within.

4. ויצו.

5. See the next chapter for Radak's explanation of the fact that Adam was created outside the Garden.

6. להתעדן implies indulgence.

7. Compare Koheles where Shlomo HaMelech makes the sun (תחת השמש) the villain in so many of the frustrations which he describes with so much sorrow.

8. שמש צדקה.

8: THE GARDEN OF EDEN III

1. See Radak there, הוא לבדו יאכל מפיריו ותולדותיו **אם יזכה הוא והם**.

2. See previous chapter.

9: THE GARDEN OF EDEN IV

1. We have purposely avoided the English equivalent. Sadly, it has become fraught with too many ugly associations.

2. Commentators point out that there was no need to bring the domesticated animals to Adam since these would have been with him all the time.

3. קרא.

4. כל נפש חיה אשר יקרא לו האדם הוא שמו.

5. See chapter 5 in detail.

6. Ramban offers the thought that the Ribono shel Olam did not want to take the woman from Adam's body until he himself would realize that he could not possibly find his partner from among the animals. Once more, we see from this Ramban that, in Adam's mind, there was a serious expectation that he could find fulfillment from among the beasts.

10: BACK TO EDEN

1. For example, the Torah uses "*orlah*" to describe the fruits which grow in the first three years of a tree's life. These fruits are forbidden to us. They are, so to speak, blocked off from us.

2. סמך, *to bring close.*

3. סמך in its נפעל, *passive* form.

4. שיהיה לבבכם פתוח לדעת האמת.

12: A VULTURE'S LOVE

1. I have probably disappointed various readers by rendering the Hebrew *nesher* as *vulture* rather than *eagle*. We admire the soaring eagle but vultures have a very bad press. However, Dr. Feliks argues persuasively that it must be the vulture which is meant. Iyov 39:30 says of the *nesher* that he is to be found wherever carrion is lying around. Eagles never eat carrion, vultures do. Dr. Feliks argues that the bird is probably called *nesher* (from *noshar*, to fall out) because its naked neck creates the impression as though the feathers had fallen out from there.

In our context, the vulture is even more useful to us than is the popular eagle. We like the eagle and expect it to be caring of its young. That even the "cruel" vulture can be so considerate of the little ones makes the picture that much more poignant.

2. קן is, of course, a nest. However, in the present context it surely means *those which inhabit the nest*.

3. The passage recalls Ramban to Bereishis 3:8. There, God reveals Himself to Adam and Chavah after they had sinned. He comes to them לרוח היום, *with the evening breeze*. Normally, as is attested in various other contexts, God's appearance takes place accompanied by a tempest. Here the Ribono shel Olam came with a pleasant, unthreatening breeze in order that Adam and Chavah should not be afraid.

4. I am not quite sure whether we have here a description of the mother or the father. Certainly the verbs *yair, yerachef, yifros, yiso'eihu, yikocheihu* are all in the masculine. Still, it seems likely that the passage describes the mother. It could be that the masculine is used either because *nesher*, the masculine form, is used for both the male and the female or because the word-picture is focused on the mighty bird (masculine attribute) which becomes soft and caring in its capacity as a mother.

5. The Iyov passage which we referenced in note 1 makes much of the wild mountains among which the *nesher* makes its home.

6. This last sentence is based on Chagigah 5b. We will be examining this Gemara in greater detail in the next chapter.

7. Yirmiyahu's prophecies are entirely suffused with visions of destruction (Bava Basra 14b).

13: HESTER PANIM

1. I admit that I owe the formulation I used here to John Donne's famous lines:

> *Each man's death diminishes me,*
> *For I am involved in mankind.*
> *Therefore, send not to know*
> *For whom the bell tolls,*
> *It tolls for thee.*

How true his sentiments were for the rest of mankind I do not know. While the tolling bells certainly do not resonate with us, his immortal observation that *No man is an island* certainly should. We do not have to look to Donne to teach us the concept of Klal Yisrael. Nevertheless, it is true that we can enhance the power of even mighty thoughts to influence us, if we present them in memorable language. These are strong lines and we can surely adopt their message in the spirit of *chochmah bagoyim ta'amin*, that we are to acknowledge that wisdom is not found only among ourselves.

14: THE DIFFERENT FACES OF *HESTER PANIM*

1. I have inserted this phrase in order to make an important point. In the event that an Amora said one thing and then another Amora is quoted, the language of the Gemara will indicate whether the second Amora is arguing with the first one or if he is just adding another point. *Rabbi X said . . .* implies a disagreement. It is to be read, Rabbi X, *on the other hand*, taught such and such. *Said Rabbi X . . .* , is an addition to what was already said but does not imply an argument.

Accordingly, the language used in our *sugia* implies that Rav Yosef is arguing with Rava. God will not communicate in a dream but will *instead* stretch out His arm over us. Turei Even does not see any disagreement between the two Amora'im and emends the text. Instead of, *Rav Yosef said . . .* he suggests that we should read, *Said Rav Yosef. . . .*

However, a number of the commentators which are available to me reject this emendation and accept the text as printed. This, of course, obligates them to find a point of disagreement between Rava and Rav Yosef. I have inserted this phrase to make clear that, in one way or another, we are faced with a disagreement the details of which have to be disentangled.

2. I am going to leave *Kenesses Yisrael* untranslated. It is easy enough to offer a literal translation, *Congregation of Israel* (Kenesses is built from the root *konos*, "to gather") but, as Chazal use it, it seems to connote something more special than that. Specifically, as in the example from Pesachim which we quote within (and there are many other instances scattered about *shas* just like this one), the purely abstract concept is reified and endowed with the faculty of speech. *Kenesses Yisrael* is, as it were, the soul or personality of the Jewish people making representations to the Ribono shel Olam. It is an idea more than a collection of people. As a unit, it is God's partner in bringing Creation to the fulfillment which the Ribono shel Olam had had in mind for it.

3. This is based on the unusual translation of Tehilim 29:4 suggested by Henry Bieberfeld in his *David King of Israel*.

15: WHEN THISTLES GROW IN GOD'S VINEYARD

1. In order to affirm *hashgachah* we must accept that there is a God, that He is aware of what happens on earth, that He cares about it and that, since He is the Creator, He has the power to direct what happens. The referenced Ramban discusses these preconditions earlier on in the same piece which we are about to analyze.

16: THE RIBONO SHEL OLAM IS WITH US—ALWAYS

1. מפני שאם איננו בוטח באלהים בוטח בזולתו ומי שבוטח בזולת ה' מסיר האלהים השגחתו מעליו ומניח אותו ביד מי שבטח עליו.

2. תרעה from רעה, *to look after sheep*.

3. תרביץ from רבץ, *to crouch down*.

4. Throughout Megillas Koheles, life, when it is narrow, unproductive and frustrating, is described as being lived *tachas hashemesh*, beneath the sun. I have

discussed the reason, based upon Maharal, in my book *Shelter Amongst the Shadows*.

5. For the purpose of our analysis we will limit our enquiry to the relationship which the Ribono shel Olam has with His chosen people. Certainly, it would be legitimate to expand our interest to encompass all of mankind, but within the framework of our interest in this chapter, we lose nothing by being less ambitious.

17: A VISIT TO THE DOCTOR'S OFFICE

1. I am not particularly satisfied with this rendering. Ramban uses "רבים," which could describe a community as well as a national entity. I chose "national entity" because, in the course of his presentation, in a section which I have not quoted here, Ramban makes much of the fact that Eretz Yisrael is frequently mentioned in connection to *rabim*. The implication is certainly that "רבים" describes the Jewish people living its national life in Eretz Yisrael.

However, the story of R. Yosef cited above which Ramban quotes contradicts the assumption that Jews must live in Eretz Yisrael for the Ramban's thesis to be true. R. Yosef lived in Babylonia and not in Eretz Yisrael. Nevertheless under Rabba's leadership when the spiritual level of the people was high, R. Yosef did not feel it necessary to summon doctors to his home.

At this point of my investigation, I am unable to reconcile these various statements.

2. I have translated PEOPLE OUGHT NOT TO DEPEND on the basis of Rashi who renders, לא היה להם לעסוק ברפאות. I have checked my search program for the phrase אין דרכן של בני אדם, which occurs quite frequently in *shas* and in every single case except for this one the translation is clearly *they* DO *not*, not *they* OUGHT *not to do*. Now it is of course clear that Rashi chose to render as he does because the context demands it. Later on in this essay, I hope to suggest a different translation which would permit this phrase to be understood in precisely the same way as it is used in all other instances.

3. Shemos 21:19. The context is the obligation of the person who is guilty of battery to reimburse his victim for the cost of the victim's required medical treatment.

4. In the course of his remarks, in a section which I have not quoted, Ramban refutes this proof. He notes that the verse does not permit the patient to seek a cure; only for the doctor to treat the patient once he is asked to do so. I do not understand why Ramban raises this question and offers an answer, without pointing out that the Gemara itself (through Abbaye) addresses this issue.

I have purposely used the word "refute" to underline this problem. It seems to me that Ramban would normally have identified his question as one which Abbaye in fact raises. He could then present his answer as a way in which Rav Acha might have defended himself.

5. See Rambam in the final chapter of the Shemonah Perakim for his discussion of the workings of gravity.

18: MIRACLES ARE NOT FOR EVERYONE

1. בכל לבבך ובכל נפשך.

2. See the discussion in chapter 16.

3. The Devarim passage does not say this in so many words, but since the passage

never mentions the eventuality that the community might in certain circumstances be left to its own devices, this persuades me that indeed this will never happen.

19: REASSESSING RAMBAN'S POSITION

1. עת פקודתם.

2. סעורן בישתהון.

3. Targum frequently uses the root סער, for the Hebrew פקד. For example, for פוקד עון אבות, *He visits the sins of the fathers [upon the children]*, he has מסער חובי.

4. Here is a quote from Ramban's commentary to Iyov which expands upon this concept:

עד כי החסיד הגמור **הדבק באלהיו** תמיד ולא יפרד הדבק במחשבתו בו בעניני מעניני העולם, יהיה נשמר תמיד מכל מקרי הזמן, אפילו ההוים בטבע, וישתמר מהם בנס יעשה לו תמיד, כאלו יחשב מכת העליונים אינם מבני ההויה וההפסד למקרי העתים, וכפי **קרבתו להדבק באלהיו ישתמר שמירה מעולה**, והרחוק מן הא"ל במחשבתו ובמעשיו, ואפילו לא יתחייב מיתה בחטאו אשר חטא, יהיה משולח ונעזב למקרים.

One who is a *chasid* in the real sense of the word, such that he cleaves to his God constantly and does not permit his mind ever to wander away to deal with worldly matters, such a one will always be protected from any harm that might overtake him because of the vagaries of nature. Miracles will be performed for him as though he belonged among the creatures that people the upper spheres, who are never subject to natural law. . . . However, one who is far away from the Ribono shel Olam in thought and deed, even if he has not committed any sin which would carry the death penalty, will be subordinated to the vagaries of nature.

5. שויתי ה' לנגדי תמיד, כי מימיני בל אמוט, *I have set HaShem before me always. Since He is at my right hand, I shall not falter.*

6. I have heard a story concerning the Brisker Rov זצ"ל. At one point, he had to make his escape by walking through an area which was teeming with Nazis. He made sure to concentrate upon the phrase אין עוד מלבדו, *There is none besides Him* and was able to make his way undetected.

20: GOD'S CHASIDIM

1. For the most part. The exception is עת פקדתם; see chapter 19.

2. God's knowledge of our physical world, that is, the providence which He dispenses, is limited to maintaining the universal rather than the individual. Even individual humans [as opposed to humanity as a whole] are subject to happenstance [literally *left to (the vagaries of) happenstance*] until the time when their fate will be visited upon them. However, [this is true of only ordinary people]. His *chasidim*, that is the most pious ones, are different. God considers them and is concerned for them even as individuals. He never for a moment relaxes his guardianship over them. . . .

3. At this point I recommend a refresher glance at chapter 19. The surface harshness of this paragraph can use a little softening.

4. Perhaps at this point you might want to glance back at chapter 4 where we discuss Ramban's interpretation of בשגם הוא בשר.

5. To get the full flavor of this passage in the Ikarim, it is important to understand the context in which the first prohibition against murder (Bereishis 9:6) is mentioned. It comes as part of the passage in which the Ribono shel Olam informs Noach that since it was in his merit that the animals were saved from the *mabul*

(see Ramban there), he would from now on be permitted to kill animals in order to eat them. It is there that the Ribono shel Olam lays down the law that *He who sheds human blood shall have his own blood shed because man was created in the image of God.* Ikarim interprets the "image of God" as indicating individual worth. God is "one" and, in a certain sense, so is man. Therefore, although under the new dispensation Noach would now be permitted to kill animals, he was not allowed to kill a fellow human.

6. Since the human part (read נשמת חיים) preponderates.

7. Since the animal part (read עפר מן האדמה) preponderates.

8. A little further along, Ramban is even more brutally frank: אבל בני אדם יושבי
הקצוות הרחוקות, שלא למדו תורה ולא ראו ישראל ואת מנהגם ... בהמות גמורות הם.

EPILOGUE

1. Please note that the moment in which we stood at Sinai was the moment that God fulfilled His promise, ולקחתי אתכם לי לעם, *I will take you as My people.* See Ramban, Shemos, chapter 25, introduction to Terumah.

2. The laws of *eved Ivri* apply only when the majority of the Jewish people reside in Eretz Yisrael, בזמן שהיובל נוהג.

3. ממלכת כהנים וגוי קדוש.

4. בשעה שבא נחש על חוה הטיל בה זוהמא ישראל שעמדו על הר סיני פסקה זוהמתן.

5. This would explain why, as Ramban sees it, Mishpatim was included in Sefer HaBris, the Book of the Covenant, in Mishpatim (Shemos 24:7). See Ramban there, 24:1.

6. The late, saintly Rav Moshe Feinstein explained why this *perek,* rather than one which had more practical relevance to the children's lives, let us say something in Maseches Shabbos, was chosen. He argued that when the children first begin to learn, they cover relatively little ground, and what they do learn they review many, many times. By learning *sugios* which deal with the marketplace, with claim and counterclaim, they will, by dint of the constant *chazarah*, absorb the truth, so important to them throughout their lives, that what belongs to Reuven does not belong to Shimon, that ownership is ownership and that taking what does not belong to you is forbidden. It is during these early years that the basis for an honest business life is laid. There is nothing, said Rav Moshe, that is more important than that.

My thinking in this essay is entirely based upon Rav Moshe's profound wisdom, although I will suggest a slightly different lesson which we all can learn from *Eilu Metzios.*

7. To forestall criticism, I state for the record that I am not taking sides. Maybe my protagonist should have gone to the graduation. If you think so, please let him know.

8. Please see the previous note.

9. I apologize to those of you who have learned *Eilu Metzios* and have picked up some of the inaccuracies in this account. Among them is the fact that if the animal's upkeep would eventually amount to more than its value, your obligation would be to sell it (try some of your colleagues at the office). My purpose here was not to paint a halachically perfect picture but to give a sense of the absolutely unimaginable sacrifices which the Torah can and does demand of us in order to return a lost object to its owner.

10. אמר רבי אלעזר שנשתייר על פכין קטנים מכאן לצדיקים שחביב עליהם ממונם יותר מגופם וכל
כך למה לפי שאין פושטין ידיהן בגזל.

11. I tried this out on my wife the other day. We had just completed our move to a new apartment. When we were finally there I said that we will have to go back because I just remembered that we had left three plastic forks there. I leave the rest of the conversation to your imagination.

12. I have used the term "Torah law" because after the famous *pruzbul* ordinance promulgated by Hillel, the requirement that the debts be remitted has *in practice* more or less lapsed. This ordinance prescribes that the creditor can protect himself from the loss of his money by executing a document, a *pruzbul*, which makes it possible for him to collect the debt indefinitely. We will be discussing the legal rationale and the ethical propriety of executing a *pruzbul* in the course of this essay.

13. However, see Chinuch 477 for some other explanations.

14. The ordinance makes *legal* sense. The wording in the Torah is such that the interdiction against pursuing the loan is addressed exclusively to the creditor. The effect of the *pruzbul* is that the loan is handed over to the courts and that therefore it is they, not the creditor, who demand payment. Clearly, the *pruzbul* does impeccably what it is supposed to do. The right to pass such an ordinance is vested in the general principle that הפקר ב"ד הפקר, which means that whatever is declared ownerless by the court is indeed ownerless. In practical terms this means that the courts can force the debtor to pay a (former) debt of which he had already been relieved by the Torah.

Nevertheless, if the rationale of the Torah's disposition is to help needy debtors, then with all its legal dressing, the ordinance still frustrates the Torah's wish. The Ribono shel Olam had wanted that the debtor should be freed of his obligation and Hillel decided that he would not be free. Why would Hillel do this?

15. While this particular aspect of the *hashmatas kesafim* law is not the focus of this essay, I cannot just pass it by without noting the enormity of this prohibition. Can we imagine a banker being approached for a loan which he knows will automatically be canceled next week? It puts a new spin on the old expression, *es iz schver tzu sein a Yid*!

If we think about it, this *halachah* is of a piece with the other *halachos* which we are discussing in this essay.

16. Together with Hillel's *takanah* of the *pruzbul*, the Mishnah (Gittin 3:4) lists another one. It provides for witnesses to a transaction to sign on the document and not to rely on their ability to testify orally. Oral testimony should really be sufficient, but there is always the possibility that the witness might not be available when their testimony is required. Much better that they sign the document and that would then be used as testimony and would not require their physical presence.

17. עשיר ברשים ימשול ועבד לוה לאיש מלוה.

18. Some of you may have noticed that I am taking the entire phrase בעל משה ידו as the subject of the verse, which is not how Rashi takes it. I will deal with this in the Appendix.

19. E.g., "I have a frog in my throat."

20. It is particularly revealing that Nechemiah 10:32 speaks of a debt as משא כל יד. Now משא (written with an א) for debt is clearly related to the verb נשה (written with a ה). משא with a ה also means *a burden*. The implication is that נשה looks at money that is owed as constituting a *burden* upon the debtor.

21. Literally, *the second tithe*. A Jewish farmer who brings in his harvest cannot simply use it as is. His first obligation is to give a portion of it (approximately

one fiftieth) to a *kohen* (*terumah*) and then a tenth of what is left to a *levi* (*maaser rishon*). That done, he must separate another tithe (*maaser sheini*) which he keeps for himself but which he may eat only in Yerushalayim. This is true for only the first, second, fourth and fifth years of the *shmitah* cycle. In the third and sixth years, he still has to tithe his produce a second time, but in those years, instead of taking it to Yerushalayim and eating it himself, he is obliged to give it to the poor (*maaser ani*).

22. See previous note.

23. When an *eved Ivri*, a Jewish slave, has served his term and makes his way to freedom, it is obligatory for the master to give him a parting gift in appreciation for the work which he has done.

24. See previous note.

25. העניק תעניק.

26. ענק.

27. אם כסף תלוה את עמי את העני עמך לא תשימון עליו נשך.

28. והדרך צלח רכב על דבר אמת וענוה צדק ותורך נוראות ימינך.

APPENDIX TO CHAPTER 3

1. It cannot be that it was pushed forward to Friday so that the Shabbos rest would not be desecrated by the creative act. If that were the case, it would be wrong to say that it would have been "ראוי" to be done on Shabbos. Clearly nothing that carries the stigma of מלאכה could have been contemplated for Shabbos.

Our assertion that we are talking of the creation of man in his ideal form, the "Shabbosdicker Yid," puts us on the right track.

In a celebrated passage, Rav Hutner ל"צז explains that even God's constant renewal of the Creation (המחדש בטובו בכל יום תמיד מעשה בראשית) does not violate the Shabbos. On that day in which the spirit preponderates, the physical world is completely subordinated to it and has no standing in its own right. Accordingly, no מלאכה takes place since only the physical can be designated by that name.

That, too, would have been the case with ideal man created on Shabbos. His physical nature would have been conceived as merely a garment to the soul and, as such, would not have been subject to the strictures of מלאכה.

APPENDIX TO THE EPILOGUE

1. This is how R. Dovid Tzvi Hoffman understands Rashi, but it does not accord with the Maharik's understanding which is quoted in the Toras Chaim Chumashim. It appears to me that R. Hoffman's interpretation fits more naturally into Rashi's language, since the Maharik makes no allowance for the "את" in "את ידו" since that clearly introduces a direct object.

2. Since the third person feminine in the future tense is always identical with the second person masculine, and since, moreover, the body parts such as יד are feminine, the translation could also be, *let your hand withdraw*. Moreover the תֵּשְׁמֵט of verse 3 is also remarkable in view of the fact that it is in *hiphil* rather than in *kal* (תִּשְׁמוֹט) as we would have expected in view of the fact that verse 2 uses שמט in the *kal*.

3. Note that throughout the Torah, Targum uses רש to render the concept of being owed money. See, for example, Shemos 22:24.

4. We need to think about verse 4, אפס כי לא יהיה בך אביון . . . . See R. Dovid Tzvi Hoffman for a careful analysis. His conclusion is that אפס here means the same as

it means throughout the Torah, "*however.*" The *pasuk* stresses that all this will not be necessary when Israel is conscientious about keeping the Torah's commandments. Then there will be no poor people and the issue of canceling the loans in the *shmitah* year will not arise.

IN RECOGNITION OF A

GENEROUS CONTRIBUTION

IN MEMORY

OF

Dr. Richard

&

Regina Weinberger

OF

VIENNA, AUSTRIA

&

BALTIMORE, MARYLAND

IN LOVING MEMORY

OF

Solomon Ralph Bijou

FROM

HIS WIFE, CHILDREN,

GRANDCHILDREN

AND

GREAT-GRANDCHILDREN

IN LOVING MEMORY

OF

Ezra & Zekia
Shasho

AND

Frieda Kredy

Albert Hamway זצ"ל

UNDERSTOOD WHAT JEWISH LIVING

WAS ALL ABOUT.

IN FARAWAY JAPAN HE RAISED HIS CHILDREN

WITH A LOVE FOR THEIR TRADITION.

THEY EACH BUILT

WARM AND LOVING JEWISH HOMES,

PASSING ON TO THEIR CHILDREN AND

THEY TO THEIRS THE FLAME

WHICH THEIR FATHER HAD PASSED TO THEM.

HE IS REMEMBERED WITH LOVE BY

HIS WIFE, HIS CHILDREN,

GRANDCHILDREN, AND GREAT-GRANDCHILDREN.

WITH HEARTS FILLED

WITH JOY

AND GRATITUDE TO HASHEM

WE

WELCOME

THE TWO NEWEST AND CUTEST

MEMBERS OF OUR FAMILY

Rachelle Zekiah

AND

Alice

— SABA AND SAVTA

מציבים אנו בזה

מזכרת נצח

לאבינו מורנו היקר

ר' לטמן

בן ר' חיים דוב בער ז"ל

איש צנוע

שכל חייו רץ כצבי

לעשות רצון אבינו שבשמים

ולאמנו מורתנו היקרה

רות רבקה לאה

בת ר' אברהם ע"ה

יהא זכרם ברוך

IN LOVING MEMORY

OF

OUR PARENTS

Mollie

AND

Sam E. Levy

❧

IN LOVING MEMORY

OF MY BELOVED PARENTS,

AND MORE,

MY GOOD AND PRECIOUS FRIENDS

Jack & Jeanette

Feldman

THEY WERE GENEROUS, WARMHEARTED,

AND GENTLE.

YOU COULD NOT MEET THEM

WITHOUT BEING TOUCHED BY THEIR

GOODNESS.

WITH A SMILE ON HIS WISE FACE

AND NOVHARDOK MUSSAR IN HIS HEART

HaRav
Chaim Mordechai
Weinkrantz זצ״ל

UNDERSTOOD US ALL SO WELL, SO VERY WELL

NO PROBLEM BUT HIS WISDOM FOUND A

SOLUTION.

NO PAIN BUT HIS EMPATHY WAS A HEALING BALM.

CHILD OF A CULTURE VERY DIFFERENT FROM

OUR OWN, HE NEVERTHELESS FOUND

COMMONALITY IN HIS AND OUR JEWISH HEARTS.

WE WILL NEVER FORGET THE BOOKS WHICH HE

SO DILIGENTLY TAUGHT US NOR THE LIFE LESSONS

FOR WHICH HE WAS A LIVING TEXT.

—THE MONDAY SHIUR